MILLINERY

BY

VIOLET BRAND

VISITING LECTURER (NEEDLE SUBJECTS) NATIONAL TRAINING COLLEGE, LONDON
LECTURER IN NEEDLEWORK, MUNICIPAL TRAINING COLLEGE, BRIGHTON
EXTERNAL EXAMINER, UNIVERSITIES OF MANCHESTER AND LIVERPOOL
EXAMINER, UNIVERSITY OF LONDON

AND

BEATRICE MUSSARED

FORMERLY TEACHER OF NEEDLEWORK, CITY TECHNICAL SCHOOL FOR WOMEN, LIVERPOOL
LECTURER IN NEEDLEWORK, ST. PETER'S COLLEGE, PETERBOROUGH
AND DIOCESAN TRAINING COLLEGE, BRIGHTON

This Bramcost Publications edition is an unabridged republication
of the rare original work.

www.BramcostPublications.com

ISBN 10: 1-934268-50-X
ISBN 13: 978-1-934268-50-6

Library of Congress Control Number: 2008926073

Bramcost
Publications

PREFACE

PREPARED originally as a notebook for our own students of millinery, it is hoped that this course will be of use to teachers, to students, to members of Women's Institutes, and to the housewife who is interested in the subject. The book is in no sense to be considered as an encyclopaedia of millinery.

The great difficulty in compiling a small and inexpensive book on such a subject lies in the fickleness of Dame Fashion. The illustrations in a book of this type tend to be even slightly out of date by the time that the book is published. For this reason, the authors have endeavoured to keep to diagrams in the text, and have added a supplement containing what might be termed topical illustrations and notes. This will be revised and renewed from time to time as fashions change and need newer illustration.

The authors would like to offer their thanks to Miss Quick, of the National Training College, Westminster, London, who may be able to find traces of her careful training throughout the book.

VIOLET BRAND.

BEATRICE MUSSARED.

CONTENTS

CHAPTER I

CHAPTER II

CHAPTER III

CHAPTER IV

CHAPTER V

CONTENTS

MILLINERY

CHAPTER I

APPARATUS USEFUL IN HOME MILLINERY

Hat Blocks.

WOODEN. Bought in various head sizes from a wholesale milliner and also from shops specializing in dress-stands. They vary in quality, some being hand-turned and shaped more carefully to the shape of the head. These are naturally more expensive and especially useful for caps and toques which fit the outline of the head closely. A wooden spinner may be bought at the same time to place under the block. It is a great convenience but not a necessity.

METAL. Bought from wholesale milliners. They are cast in metal alloy and are hollow. They can therefore be placed over a gas ring. This is a quicker method for blocking crowns, and dispenses with the necessity of using a flat iron. These are not as well shaped at the forehead and nape of the neck as a good wooden block, and the worker must be careful not to allow the brim to scorch if the brim and crown are blocked in one piece.

CORK BLOCKS, or wig-makers' blocks. These are light in weight and pins may be stuck into them, but they require care or they chip badly.

EXPANDING BLOCKS are really designed for the purpose of stretching hats and are of little use for blocking. When expanded they must be covered by a rubber cap, but even so the hat tends to sink in the centre.

HOME-MADE BLOCKS may be made from an old straw crown filled with torn paper. A pudding basin may be well padded with cotton wool until it is an oval shape and then covered with material.

RUBBER CAPS FOR BLOCKS may be obtained so that one block will do for a larger size. They are expensive, cut easily, and will not stand heat, therefore a cheap felt will do just as well.

FELT ROLL. A triangle of felt or fine blanket about 10 in. base measure. Roll very tightly from the apex and sew in position. Most useful for a pad when pressing, as it is thick in the middle and thin at each end. Illustrated on page 7.

WIRE PLIERS, with cutting edge. Choose these with pointed noses. They may be obtained from a metal worker's tool shop.

KNIVES FOR CUTTING FELT. A penknife or razor blade achieves the best result. Felt must be cut evenly and steadily and clean through at the first attempt. Scissors flatten the edge and tend to produce a jagged effect.

MILLINERY PINS. Fine steel pins about 2 in. long. Obtainable by ¼ lb. box at a good haberdashers. Keep them in the black paper in which they are packed to prevent rusting. A prick from a rusty pin causes septic fingers. If pins become rusty, soak in paraffin and wipe dry.

BRIM IRONS. Used by some workers but not a necessity. Shaped like a banana, with a long handle. The "Banana" part is heated on gas. May also be obtained electrically heated. The round edge is useful to iron inside a curved-up brim. (See illustrations in supplement.)

Stiffening Agents.

GUM ARABIC. Bought in crystals from a chemist. The brown crystals should be removed for light coloured work. Place the crystals in a wide-mouthed jar and cover with cold water. Leave twenty-four hours or more. Strain through muslin and bottle for use. Used in the water in blocking felts or straws which require to be given a little stiffness and which if varnished would be too shiny. The proportion of gum required varies with the type of hood to be stiffened and the stiffness desired.

STARCH. Used for linen hats. Mix as for cold water starch, and use when blocking or for the brim only.

GUM TRAGACANTH. Obtained from a chemist. Expensive but very clear, therefore good for fine material such as lace, flowers, ribbons, white hats, etc.

GELATINE. Ordinary powdered kitchen variety. Useful for open-work straws such as crochet, as the mixture "sets" in the holes. About 3 measures to a pint of warm water. Dip the hat while the mixture is warm and block immediately before it sets. If the colour is liable to run, dissolve a lump of kitchen salt in the water first.

CRYSTAL STIFFENING bought from wholesale milliners. Use according to directions.

MILLINERY VARNISH. Either clear or dark can be obtained from a wholesale milliner. Apply with a stiff brush when the hat is perfectly dry. Work quickly in a warm room or the varnish may "streak." Begin from the top of a crown for a straw, taking care to work the varnish well into the straw and not to go over the same place twice. When the outside is dry, varnish the underbrim if extra stiffness is required. This must be done before lining or trimming.

For felt hats with large brims, paint the underbrim with varnish. Test a scrap of felt to see that it will not dry white after varnishing, in which case use gum in the blocking water.

RUBBER SOLUTION. Similar to cycle tyre mending solution, this is obtainable from wholesale milliners, in 2-lb. or 2-oz tins. Tins should be kept closed or the mixture dries up. Apply with an old knife or a stick, and spread it like thin treacle. It is used to stick seams on straw, and for sticking straw insets into felt, petersham ribbon, tips of headlinings, feather pads to crowns, flowers, etc.

Materials Used.

ESPARTRA OR SPARTERIE. Made from Esparto grass which grows in Spain, Japan, and South America. It is woven and stuck to stiff muslin and used to make shapes which are to be covered with material; also as headbands inside straws and felts. Very light and wears well. There are two kinds and three degrees of stiffness obtainable. It is bought by the sheet which measures about 30 in. × 24 in. French. The best quality. Stiff used for large brims. Medium for general use. Soft for stretched espartra brims and toques. The soft kind is not so easy to handle. Japanese. In one quality only. It frays more easily than the French, is more brittle, and is not so easy to use, but is cheaper.

BUCKRAM. Is bought by the yard in white or black, 36 in. wide, and used for hat shapes. This is stiff and difficult to use. Produces a hard effect. Wears badly as it will not stand any rain. Cheaper than espartra.

MILLINERY CANVAS. Bought by the yard about 28 in. and 42 in. wide, natural colour, from a wholesale milliner. Used for stitched crossway shapes and under tweed materials.

MILLINERY NET. 24 in. wide, bought by the yard from wholesale milliners. White and black and some colours, and in three degrees of stiffness: coarse, medium, and fine. Used for blocked crowns (see Chapter III, p. 23) and for mounting transparent materials and trimmings.

BOOK MUSLIN. Bought at a draper's in white and black 35 in. 36 in. wide. Stiffer and more opaque than Leno muslin. Used for blocking (see Millinery Net above), and for interlining the brims of linen hats.

DOMETTE. Bought from a draper by the yard. There are two kinds. French 52 in. to 54 in., in black or white like open fluffy stockinette, very elastic.

English in white and black 31 in. wide, more like a loose flannel. Used for interlining under thin silks in covering shapes (see Chapter IV, page 26) and babies' bonnets.

BUTTER MUSLIN. A soft muslin like cheese cloth; used for interlining georgettes and crêpe de Chines in white only, 36 in. wide.

PAPER WIRE. The cheapest and strongest kind used in millinery. A copper wire covered in paper. Used for flower stalks, and to wire blocks. No. 7 is extra strong.

SUPPORT WIRE. Covered in cotton in black and white only. Seldom used. Silk-covered is in general use. Runs in numbers 7 to 3. Numbers 5 to 6 usually required for shape making; 4 for firm straw work; about 7 metres in each ring of wire. No. 4 can be obtained in colours.

LACE WIRE. Numbers 2 to 00. Silk covered. Number 2 useful for fine straws. No. 0 is kept in colours.

SATIN WIRE. Wire padded with cotton strands and bound with silk, used as the headwires for wire shapes as it is very comfortable.

RIBBON WIRE. Like a wired tape. Sold on cards at the haberdashery counter. Black and white only. Used for wiring large ribbon loops. May be cut in half if too wide.

FELTS. See Chapter VI.

STRAWS. See Chapter VII.

STRAW CLOTHS. Material bought by the yard 12 in. to 18 in. wide, to imitate straw and make up over light foundations as if it were material.

CHINA RIBBON. Very narrow ribbon in white or black. Sold on cards (36 yd.) and used to draw up headlinings.

SARCENET. A thin papery silk used for headlining and usually sold only in black and white.

SILK VELVET. 18 in. or 38 in. wide. Real silk velvet curls up at the edge. It is very light. Expensive, but used by the best milliners.

PATENT OR MILLINERY VELVET. 18 in. wide. Has some cotton in it, a glazed back, and a close pile.

COTTON BACK. Cotton with an open pile 18 in. wide.

MIRROR AND PANNE VELVET. 38 in. wide. A longer pile, which is ironed flatter and so produces a satin effect.

VELVETEEN is made of cotton and is too heavy for any millinery except stitched sports hats.

NOTES ON USING VELVETS.

(i)   Note the pile. It is more becoming if the material is cut to shade dark from front to back.

(ii)   Roll the material over paper. Do not fold.

(iii) Stab the pins and use only steel ones.

(iv)   Press over an iron. Do not iron the pile down.

(v)   Use silk to tack and cut each stitch instead of pulling the tacking thread out.

(vi)   When cutting and joining on the cross, note the shading of the pile.

(vii) Some people mark velvet with their fingers; in this case make little finger stalls of velvet to wear and so hold pile with pile.

CHAPTER II

PATTERN MAKING

It is possible to buy ready-made hat patterns. The disadvantages of these are twofold: they are not always of the correct size, because heads and coiffures vary in shape beyond the actual *tour-de-tête* or head size, and further if one takes the trouble to make a hat, one usually desires an individual one—in fact "a model," or at least "a copy of the original model, madam." It is for this reason that three different methods of obtaining brim patterns are given, and the advantages and disadvantages of each are suggested so that the reader may choose the method best suited to the purpose in hand. Crowns are treated in the second section of the chapter. (See also Supplement.)

It should be realized that a flat brim of a hat is like a plate with a hole in it, and for that the worker may not require a pattern except to gauge the size of the head and to ascertain whether the width of the brim is becoming. In this connection it should be mentioned that a white paper pattern will look bigger than a dark brim in the same size.

When copying a hat from an illustration or photograph, the worker will be helped to judge the relative width of the brim if she compares the width of the brim with the width of the eyebrows in the illustration and then measures her own eyebrows in front of a mirror.

It should also be borne in mind that part of the brim in the illustration will be seen in perspective, and will in reality be wider than it appears. General observation of the season's styles must guide the worker here.

Method 1.

To take an exact pattern of the brim of a soft hat, fold the brim in half so that there is a fold at the centre front, and pin the head lines together. Take a double piece of paper and lay the brim with the centre front fold to the fold of the paper. Pin the fold to fold. Arrange the brim to lie flat on the paper, taking no notice of the crown. It may be possible to keep it in position with the hand, but, if the brim is large, pin the hat in position. To mark the headline on the pattern, prick through the headline of the hat with a large pin or needle and it will show on the paper underneath.

Mark the outer edge of the brim and the back join and fold, by outlining the brim with a pencil. Lift the hat model from the paper. Carefully outline the pricked headline on the paper and compare and correct the size of the headline if necessary. Correct the outer edge if necessary. Should both sides of the brim be of different widths, proceed as for the headline and prick through with a needle.

The shape of the headline varies with the different styles of hairdressing.

5

Table of Head Sizes for Women and Children's Hats

Size		Head Measures	Front to back	Side to side
		In.	In.	In.
$6\frac{1}{4}$	For small child or child . . .	$19\frac{1}{2}$	$14\frac{1}{4}$	$13\frac{1}{2}$
$6\frac{3}{8}$	For children	20	15	$14\frac{1}{4}$
$6\frac{1}{2}$		$20\frac{1}{4}$	$15\frac{1}{4}$	$14\frac{1}{2}$
$6\frac{5}{8}$		$20\frac{3}{4}$	$14\frac{1}{2}$ to $15\frac{1}{2}$	$12\frac{1}{2}$ to $15\frac{1}{2}$
$6\frac{3}{4}$	For small adults . . .	$21\frac{1}{4}$	15 to $15\frac{1}{2}$	$14\frac{1}{2}$ to 15
$6\frac{7}{8}$		$21\frac{3}{4}$	$15\frac{1}{2}$	15
7		$22\frac{1}{2}$	15 to 16	$14\frac{1}{2}$ to 15
$7\frac{1}{8}$	For adults	$22\frac{7}{8}$	15 to 16	$14\frac{1}{2}$ to 15
$7\frac{1}{4}$		$23\frac{1}{4}$	15 to 16	
$7\frac{3}{8}$	For large head size with knot of hair .	$23\frac{5}{8}$		
$7\frac{1}{2}$	For large head size with large quantity of hair	24		

For a head with hair arranged in plaits over the ears, the headline may be a circle; but for short hair or hair dressed in a knot at the back of the head, the headline must form an oval, directions for making which will be found on page 9.

The actual head measure is taken round the part of the head where the hat is worn. At the time of writing this measure is taken across the forehead and kept high across the back of the head avoiding a knot of hair if there is one; but by next year this measure may be taken low down or over one eye.

The side-to-side measure is taken over the top of the head from ear to ear, as in the illustration on page 7.

The back-to-front measure is taken from the forehead to wherever the head line comes at the back of the head.

The positions for these measures will vary with fashion, but a head measure, back-to-back and a side-to-side measure, must always be taken before a start is made on a hat, and, by looking at up-to-date fashion books and the newest hats, the worker can observe the proper positions for these measures. (See illustration in Supplement.)

Method 2.

By drafting to direct measure and pleating to obtain a turn-up or turn-down brim.

Required: A sheet of firm paper. A ruler, pencil and tape-measure. Illustration of a hat or the actual model.

Measurements Required.

	Example
Head measure	. $22\frac{1}{2}$ in.
Width of brim at centre front	. 2 in.
,, ,, ,, centre back	. $1\frac{3}{4}$ in.
,, ,, ,, right-hand side	. 2 in.
,, ,, ,, left-hand side	. $2\frac{1}{2}$ in.

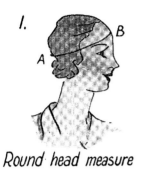

Round head measure

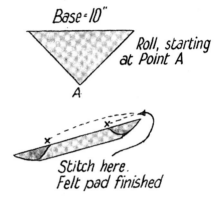

Base = 10"

Roll, starting at Point A

A

Stitch here.
Felt pad finished

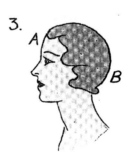

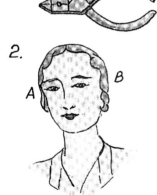

Side to side measure

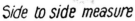

Back to front measure

Measurement at outer edge, if a model is being copied.

CONSTRUCTION LINES. Rule two lines to form a cross. Measure from centre of cross one-sixth of head measure and swing a circle with compass or piece of string. This will fit a head with hair dressed over the ears. For a shingled head: take off $\frac{1}{4}$ in. at each side and add $\frac{1}{4}$ in. at the centre front and back.

For hair dressed in a knot: take off $\frac{1}{2}$ in. at the sides and add $\frac{1}{2}$ in. at the centre front and back.

Measure the line carefully, and alter till it is exact. Use the tape measure standing on its edge to form a little wall, and so obtain an accurate measure on a curve.

THE BRIM. Measure the width of the brim from the headline at the four quarters, and draw the outer edge.

Caution: draw from the inside of the circle, because the wrist acts as a natural compass. Avoid a straight edge between the quarter marks. Cut out the pattern on both the head and outer edge line.

TO MAKE THE BRIM TURN UP OR DOWN. The outer edge must be made smaller to obtain either effect. Take in small pleats not bigger than $\frac{1}{4}$ in. in the paper pattern at the outer edge and fix with a pin in each pleat. The pleats must run out to nothing at the headline, and may be placed where the greatest amount of turn-up or droop is required. (See illustrations and Supplement.)

Try on the paper pattern and alter if required. It will, of course, look ridiculous in paper, but will serve the purpose.

TO FLATTEN THE BRIM FOR USE IN CUTTING OUT. Begin at centre front, fold the pattern in half, placing the edges of the headline together, and crease the pattern flat. The centre back may have changed at the outer edge. Cut up the new back crease, and the pattern is ready to lie flat on material. Mark the centre front by cutting a little hole or snip through the middle of the brim.

Method 3.

By working on a radius. This method is quick and suitable for classwork where a rapid result is required. It is arbitrary and allows for little individual variation. It is a suitable method for obtaining brims which turn up or down, and the worker should note that the greater the radius XA the more will the hat turn up or down. Diagram and notes will be found on page 9. The size given in the diagram will form a tricorne when ironed or wired into shape.

Crowns.

When designing crowns, the height and proportions of the entire figure, and especially the skirt length should be considered. Crowns may be anything ranging from the simplest form, which consists of a circle of material 13 in. to 16 in. in diameter, pleated or gathered to fit the headband, to a complicated seamed or draped crown which requires keen observation to design, and practice to make up.

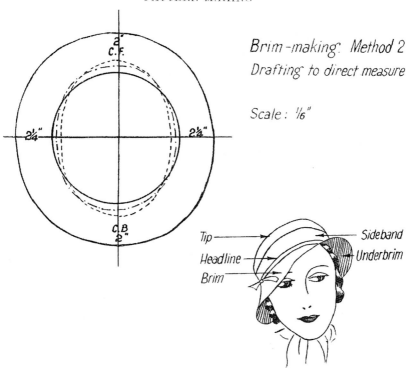

Brim-making. Method 2
Drafting to direct measure

Scale : ⅙"

Tip
Headline
Brim

Sideband
Underbrim

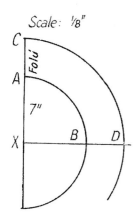

Scale: ⅛"

Brim-making. Method 3
*Turn-up or -down Brim obtained
by means of a radius.*
X = Centre
XA = 7 in = about ⅓rd. total Head measure.
Swing a radius X-A
A-B = ½ Head-measure, measured on Curve.
A-C = Width of Brim. Swing a radius from X-C.
Rule a line through X, B, D.
B-D = Back Seam.

1. A Crown Made in Two Parts. Similar to the illustration on brim pattern page 9, may be made in two parts—tip and sideband.

The tip pattern consists of the oval cut out of the centre of the brim.

The sideband may be about 3 in. deep for a hat as illustrated, but may range from $2\frac{1}{2}$ in. to 5 in. according to fashion. The length will equal the head

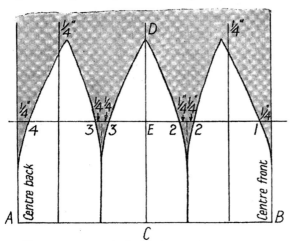

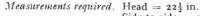

Measurements required. Head = $22\frac{1}{2}$ in.
　　　　　　　　　　　 Side to side = $14\frac{1}{2}$ in.
　　　　　　　　　　　 Front to back = 15 in.

These measures must be taken carefully on the wearer as directed, page 7.

Construction lines. AB = $\frac{1}{2}$ head measure rule. A = centre-front. B = centre-back.

　　　AC = $\frac{1}{2}$ AB. Rule a line at right angles to AB line = to $\frac{1}{2}$ side to side measure = D.

　　　CE = $\frac{1}{2}$ CD line. Raise the same line at centre-front and centre-back.

　　　Rule a line from centre-front to centre-back parallel to headline and passing through E.

Pattern lines. Divide AB into thirds to make three sections. Find the centre of each and rule a guiding line = CD in length.

Side sections CD = centre. Curve the seam to pass $\frac{1}{4}$ in. inside at the line E.

Front section. To obtain the extra length shift the point of the section $\frac{1}{4}$ in. to the left at the same level.

　　　Curve the section as before $\frac{1}{4}$ in. inside the guiding line.

Back section. Draw in the same as the front but shift the point to the right.

　　　Note that the lines of the sections must not bulge at all.

measure plus 1 in., and is usually ruled with pencil or chalk straight on to the material. It may be cut as a paper pattern, but as it is invariably cut on the cross keep the seam slanting so that the join will be on the straight thread (see the illustration for cutting out, page 13).

2. A Moulded Crown. May be cut in the same fashion and treated as described in Chapter III, pages 21, 22.

3. DRAPED CROWN. A soft and becoming style, nearly always in fashion, is founded on this same pattern (for notes on this see Chapter IV, page 36).

4. SECTIONAL CROWNS. These crowns may be planned in many ways as fashion requires. The most usual are cut with 4, 6, or 8 sections. It should be noted that 4 sections give little scope for shaping, and unless the material blocks very well the result will always tend to be rather angular and like a tea-cosy. Six sections work up nicely, and may be arranged either with a seam from front to back as in the diagram and the draft, or with a section at centre front and back, and a seam from side to side. A crown with eight sections is frequently made. It is more difficult to make well, as the sections tend to be narrow at the top, and the seams need very careful management. The pattern and notes are shown on page 10.

Note that the line must not "bulge" at all, and should pass $\frac{1}{4}$ in. from the construction lines at the level E.

Measure the length of the seams very carefully before cutting out the pattern. Number the seams as in the diagram. The pattern must be quite exact or the crown will wrinkle and the labour of making up will be wasted. For making up see Chapter VIII.

In fitting, the headlines AB may need slight alteration, but if the pattern is properly made the rest should be reliable.

Sectional crowns may be divided in other ways according to fashion. To do this the reader should refer to Chapter III, page 23, and make a blocked muslin crown. Draw on the muslin the position of the seams, and mark or number the different sections. Cut up the muslin crown and use it for a pattern. Allow $\frac{1}{4}$ in. turnings when cutting out, and block the crown when it is made up, as the curves of the muslin pattern will be partly lost when it is pinned out as a pattern. (See also Supplement.)

CHAPTER III

SHAPE MAKING

Choice of Materials.

FASHION must be followed here, and the worker must look at models and keep herself up to date in this respect. Lightness and comfort must be aimed at, and judgment and experience alone will teach the worker to choose her materials so that the hat will keep its shape in wear without having that hard "upholstered" look that is sometimes achieved by otherwise good amateur workers. A list of some materials with comments is given on pages 2, 3. The standard methods of shape making are given because the methods themselves are never long out of fashion, even if they may be used on different materials and in different ways.

1. To Make a Stiff Brim Ready for Covering.

Take the materials for the brim, a sheet of espartra or buckram; silk support wire No. 5 or 6; No. 16 or 24 cotton, No. 6 straw needle; pins, scissors, wire nippers, and other sewing implements. Soft material for mulling the edge.

Place the pattern as shown in the diagram, page 13. Note that the muslin side of espartra and the smooth side of buckram are kept next to the head for comfort; and it is an invariable rule in all millinery that the centre front of all pieces is placed to the direct cross. This is probably the only permanent rule in millinery and is founded on two good reasons: firstly, that hats are pulled down vigorously on the forehead when placed on the head and need to "give" a little or they would split; and, secondly, because the cross-cut material makes the head look a better shape. Allow turnings as shown and mark the edge of the pattern on the espartra or buckram with pencil, mark the centre front through the hole in the pattern.

Lay of Pattern on French Espartra   (Scale = 1/6")

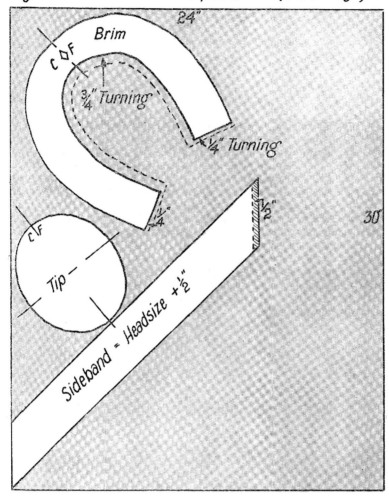

1. To Join the Brim. Overlap the two pencil marks at the centre back join. Pin in position. Thread the needle and make a knot $1\frac{1}{2}$ in. from the end of the cotton. Begin at the headline, and join the back seam by two rows of back-stitching. The stitches may be $\frac{1}{2}$ in. to $\frac{3}{4}$ in. long. Place the stitches on the side of the brim where they will show least when the hat is covered with material, on the underside for a turn-down brim, on the upper side for a turn-up brim. Work by stabbing to and fro to avoid bending the stiff material, and not by picking up a stitch as in needlework. Finish off at the headline by tying the two ends together in a reef knot. This method of beginning, joining on a new cotton, and ending off is always used in millinery, thereby avoiding back-stitches which might make holes in fragile materials. This is also the reason for strong cotton and large stitches. A useful method of preventing the espartra join showing through the covering is to "skin it," that is, to lift the muslin from the grass at the raw edge, cut away the grass for $\frac{1}{6}$ in. and stick or sew the muslin down to cover the raw edge.

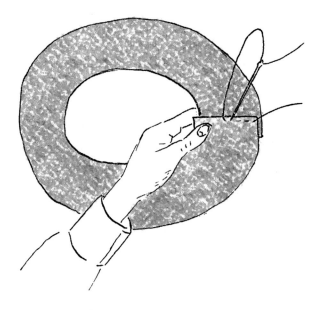

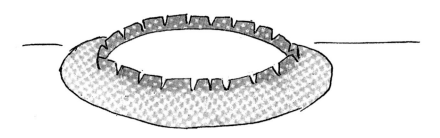

2. To Wire the Head. A hat that does not fit is useless. A $\frac{1}{4}$ in. more or less is a big amount, and an amateur easily pulls a shape in too tight while sewing; therefore test the head measure very carefully on the pencil line. Stand the tape measure like a wall and measure a very little at a time. Verify the measure. Note that if the oval is a poor shape the hat will "wave" at the edge of the brim. If it is too big, re-pencil the whole line slightly inside the circle. When correct, snip the turnings as far as the correct headline every $\frac{1}{2}$ in. (see diagram, page 15). Cut off the wire to equal the head measure plus $1\frac{1}{2}$ in. overlap; never allow less overlap, or the end will escape and pierce the covering. Begin at the back, avoiding the espartra join. Place the wire on the pencil line and fix by wire-stitch (see illustration, page 17). Wire from right to left. Hold the cotton parallel with the wire. Insert the needle on one side of the wire (by stabbing) and bring it up on one side of the wire and cotton to pass through the loop. Stitches may be $\frac{3}{8}$ in. apart.

To join a new cotton. Leave an end; begin the new cotton with a knot, as above, and tie the two ends in a reef knot. Where the wire joins, work the stitches very close together to cover the points of the wire where they overlap, then work back to the beginning and tie off the cotton with a reef knot.

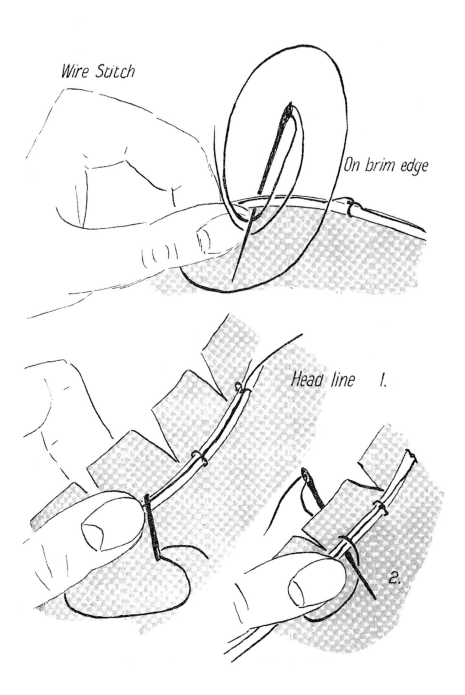

Wire Stitch

On brim edge

Head line   I.

2.

3. TO WIRE THE OUTER EDGE. Run the finger round the raw edge to fee
for anything uneven, and trim it off. For a closely turned-up hat it may be
necessary to soften the roll up by rubbing with a thimble, but it will be moulded
with the iron later. At all costs avoid cracking the espartra grass. Begin, as
before, at the centre back. For a turn-up hat, place the wire slightly on the upper
side; for a turn-down, over on the underside of the brim.

Hold the wire on the edge of the brim. Work from right to left on the knee,
not on the table, and keep the hat between the hands and chest; in this manner
the worker has more control over the work.

To fasten on, begin with a millinery knot. The stitch is a knotted stitch,
and the wire should not slip between the stitches. Work as illustrated, and
hold the cotton tight in the left hand till the last minute.

The worker must watch her model, shaping as she works. Sometimes it is
necessary to hold the wire a little tight and ease the brim edge to the wire,
so causing a more rounded turn-up. A skilful worker can do much by this
manipulation. (See Supplement illustration.)

Finish off as described above for the headline. Test the head measure.

To strengthen the headline where an espartra crown is not used, cut a crossway strip of espartra $\frac{3}{4}$ in. to 1 in. wide and equal to the head measure in length
plus $\frac{1}{2}$ in. Place this above the head wire on the outside of the turnings, and
stab-stitch the snipped turnings to it. Arrange the stitches as illustrated, page
19. This keeps the little tabs in position. The worker may tend to draw the
strip in and make the head size too small. Test the head with a tape measure
to be sure that this has not occurred.

4. TO MULL THE WIRED EDGE. Mulling is a process used to soften the edge
of the hat, and the outer cover is fixed to it on the brim. It is not necessary to
use mull muslin; any scraps of soft silk or chiffon can be used, as it will be hidden
later. Cut a crossway strip $1\frac{1}{2}$ in. wide, and pleat the strip so that it is creased
as illustrated. Note that there are three thicknesses in the centre, and two only
at each edge. Fold in half again and crease. Place the binding over the edge
of the hat, stretch it well, and fix by means of back-stitch. Use 50 or 60 cotton,
and place the long stitches where they will show least. When joining the mull
binding, avoid a lump by cutting the binding off straight. Cut the new piece
straight as well, and place the two pieces to touch but not to overlap. Hold in
place by the back-stitches.

For thick coverings such as velvet, work a row of back-stitches $\frac{1}{8}$ in. from the
outer edge of the hat. This gives something to catch the material to and is
better than the narrow mull.

To fold the mull

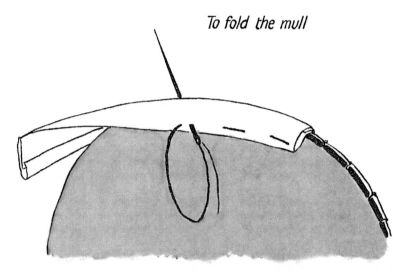

Mull binding on brim edge

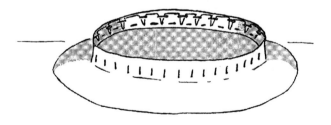

Strengthening strip at head

5. To Mould a Curved Brim by Hand, and avoid the sharp unfinished look which the paper pattern produces. Use a hot iron (light weight), a roll of felt or blanket (see illustration Chapter I) and some water. If the roll were not used to pad the brim, the iron would cause a dent and there would be nothing to press on to. Damp the brim slightly with the fingers dipped in water, or with a damp sponge. Fill the curve with the pad and grip the brim over the pad with the left hand. Place the centre of the iron (not the toe or heel) on the brim and pad, and rock it back and forward on the padded curve. Do not press hard. After some practice the worker will use the iron as easily as if it were the right hand, but to begin with it will make her wrist ache. (See Supplement illustration.)

Some workers will prefer to use a brim iron. This is obtainable from a wholesale milliner. It is somewhat of the shape of a banana, and is heated by gas or electricity. This is used inside the curve of the brim while the brim is on the blanket and the brim is gently "rubbed" into shape.

2. Crown Making.

Crown foundations may be—

(a) Of the same material as the brim, such as buckram or espartra. They are then usually either square or in two pieces moulded. Factory-made crowns are sometimes cut in one piece, but it is both extravagant and difficult for the amateur to make this.

(b) When a foundation is required for flowers, feathers, or crinoline straws, the crowns are made of lighter material, such as millinery net or book muslin, and may be blocked in one piece if desired, because it is lighter and quicker to make in this way.

(c) The making up of sectional crowns is explained in Chapter VIII, page 62.

(d) Directions for soft draped crowns will be found in Chapter IV, page 36.

(i). Crown of Espartra or Buckram. The sideband consists of a crossway strip, the length being equal to head measure plus $\frac{1}{2}$ in. overlap × 2 in. to 5 in. wide according to fashion.

Note that for a square crown the depth of the sideband is equal to the finished depth of the crown, but for a moulded crown allow $\frac{3}{4}$ in. turning at the top of the sideband. The join at the back is slanting, i.e. on the straight thread. If the crown is required to be higher at one place than at another, make the alteration in height at the top of the sideband, not at the headline. Cut the tip by the drafted pattern (see Chapter II, page 9); place the centre front to the cross, and allow $\frac{1}{2}$ in. turnings for a square crown, but none for a moulded one. Mark the outline of the pattern, and the halves and quarters on the smooth side of the espartra, with pencil.

(ii). Making up Square Crown. Join up the sideband with $\frac{1}{2}$ in. overlap, and fix by means of back-stitching, as described for the back of the brim (page 14). Wire the top edge of the sideband with lappet wire No. 2 or support wire if a covering is to be of heavy material. Test the pencil line round the tip and note that it should be the same as the top of sideband. Trim off the turnings allowed on the tip except for a tab at the four quarters. Use these tabs to pin

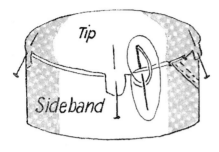

Joining tip of square crown

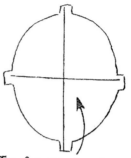

Tip for square crown

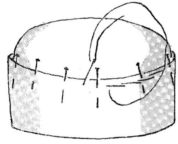

Joining tip of moulded crown

Brim and sideband in one piece before stretching

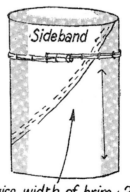

Twice width of brim + 2"

the tip in position to the sideband. Fix the tip to the sideband by wire-stitch. (See illustration page, 21.) When the tab is reached, trim it off before sewing that part of the crown. Mull the seam with a strip of mull folded as for the edge of the brim. Fix the mull by means of rows of back-stitching, using fine cotton and placing the small stitches on the outside.

The treatment of the lower edge depends on how the crown is to be covered. The raw edge of the espartra tends to fray and stretch. It may be

(a) Wired with lappet wire No. 2 and mulled, or

(b) Mulled only.

Both these methods are suitable when the crown is to be covered with a heavy type of material or when a firm hat is desired by a matron. Quick and light-fingered workers may dispense with both wire and mull, or at most use a single piece of crossway mull (leaving the raw edges of mull showing) to prevent the espartra fraying. Another method is to fix the crown to the brim straight away by means of back-stitching (long stitches on the inside); or if the brim has not had a strengthening strip added to the head then fix by the stitch illustrated by diagram on page 19.

(iii). MAKING UP A CROWN WITH MOULDED TIP. Mark the edge of the pattern and at the halves and quarters, with pencil, on the smooth side of the espartra. Join the back seam of the espartra as for the square crown above, the smooth side outside. The $\frac{3}{4}$ in. turning will be round the top. Damp this turning slightly. Place the centre front of the tip and the halves and quarters to the halves and quarters of the sideband, and pin the turning over these (see illustration, page 21). It is awkward to hold without creasing, and the chest must act as a third hand. The espartra is non-transparent, and the worker must be careful to see that the outline of the tip is cut to a perfect oval to start with, and comes exactly to the pencilled line on the sideband. Ease the sideband evenly on to the tip and pin it all round. The pins should be in an upright position. An amateur requires some practice to do this, as it is easy to get an uneven effect. The ease will tend to come at the last places pinned, and it is better to pin it roughly all round and then go round again, making it even. The muslin is apt to part from the espartra when damp. Trim away a scrap of the grass and let the muslin lie over the rough edges. Fix by two rows of back-stitching, one row close to each raw edge and the long stitches on the inside. Place the felt roll inside the crown and mould into a nice curve with a hot iron (see directions for moulding on page 20). If the covering material requires it, the seam round the tip should be mulled with a single mull (a crossway strip $\frac{1}{2}$ in. wide stretched well and left with raw edges). Fix with fine thread and small stitches on the outside. (See illustration in Supplement.)

Treat the lower edge of the crown as described for the square crown above.

It is possible to make a crown like this in millinery canvas or book muslin, but it usually saves time to make it up with the material. Directions for this are given on page 36.

Sometimes the method given above would be inconvenient because the seam might show through a thin covering. In this case, block the tip and block the sideband, allow an overlap of ¾ in. When they are dry, sew them together. Directions for blocking are given below.

(*b*). CROWNS BLOCKED IN ONE PIECE. Transparent or semi-transparent hats call for semi-transparent foundations. These can be made of blocked millinery net, book muslin or leno, used alone, or in conjunction with an espartra brim.

Crinoline and lace straws always have to be made up over a transparent foundation, as well as the small hats made entirely of flowers, or feather pads. Other types of straws may not need a whole crown foundation, but in the case of a raffia plait or any loosely woven hat, it is a great advantage to put a blocked net tip into the top of the crown, to prevent the head stretching the straw.

Millinery net can be bought in three thicknesses, fine, medium, and coarse; particulars as to widths will be found in Chapter I, page 3.

Before starting to block, rub the block with white beeswax to prevent the net sticking. If a wooden block is being used, arrange two pieces of tape from back to front and side to side. This is not necessary in the case of an aluminium block if it is well waxed.

Prepare a strip of espartra cut on the cross ¾ in. to 1 in. wide, length equal to head measure, plus 1½ in. for turnings. Join into a circle. Put it on the block exactly where the headline is to come. Pin to the tapes to prevent it slipping. The pins will have to be removed before the net dries. Cut net about 18 in. square, put it in cold water and remove without wringing. Place it over the block, a corner to centre front, centre back and sides. Tie firmly at the headline with string. Then remove any fullness by pulling down at the corners. It will be found possible to remove practically all the extra fullness by manipulation at the centre back, centre front, and sides.

Tack the net on to the headband, taking care not to catch in the tapes. Use 16–20 cotton. Cut away the superfluous net and dry quickly.

With an aluminium block the worker will find that as soon as the net is quite dry it slips off very easily with no further work.

With a wooden block, shift the tapes backwards and forwards to loosen the net. When the net is loosened it lifts off, keeping its shape perfectly, and is then ready for use. (See illustration in Supplement.)

Leno and book muslin are blocked in exactly the same way. Leno is usually used double. Two 18 in. to 20 in. squares must be cut, put together, wetted together, and put on the block together. So long as they are not worked separately they are just as easy to manage as single material.

Book muslin is very sticky when wet, owing to the large amount of stiffening it contains. It makes a very hard crown, and is really only suitable for the heavier types of straw or other covering, or for a cheap foundation such as would be required in club classes.

If the foundation is only to go in the top part of the crown there is no need to sew it to a headband when blocking. It will be cut off just above the headline before being put into the hat, or it will be found to take up too much room.

It is also possible to block a crown entirely of tulle, either as a lining for a lace straw crown, or used over a net foundation as a crown by itself. Care must be taken to buy waterproof tulle, as nothing else will block well.

Prepare the block as for millinery net and prepare a kettle of boiling water. Take a piece of tulle, fold it into layers. At least 6 or 8 layers, each 18 in. to 20 in. square, would be needed for the crown. Place over the block, tie a string round the headline, and very carefully begin to pull down the tulle into shape. No "spaces" must be left between the layers of tulle.

Then hold the block in the steam of the kettle, pulling the tulle down gently and gradually all the time, till all the extra material is eased away at the headline. Stitch the tulle to the headband. Cut off surplus material, and put the block to dry.

Any soft make of straw hat is improved with a blocked net or leno tip. Leno is usually best, as it is not as stiff as net. It prevents the top of the crown losing its shape. Draped velvet toques or berets are much improved when mounted over a light foundation. It is possible then to tie the draping and folds in position and to save having to arrange them when the hat is put on.

3. Shapes with the Brim and the Sideband in One Piece and Suitable for Small Hats.

These are made of a piece of soft or medium espartra or millinery canvas cut on the cross and stretched at one edge to form the brim.

There is a limit to the amount which a crossway strip will stretch, and therefore it is not possible to make the brim wider than about 2 in. unless the brim is turned up very much, as for a Russian toque or Tudor effect. It is a useful method for small toques for older people, or where a little brim is required to shade the eyes.

Shapes made in this way are very light in weight and extremely quickly made.

THERE ARE TWO WAYS OF MAKING THESE BRIMS.

1. WITH WIRE AT THE OUTER EDGE. Cut the espartra band to be equal to the head measure plus $\frac{1}{2}$ in. ease and $\frac{3}{4}$ in. overlap.

The width is equal to depth of sideband required, plus the greatest width of the brim, plus 2 in. turnings.

Note that a crossway strip becomes narrower when stretched. The band must lie on the direct cross. It may have two joins in it for economy, and these should be placed equally on each side of the centre back. It is better with only one join.

To make up, mark the centre front and half and quarters with pencil. Measure the depth of the sideband, and rule a line in pencil on the rough side for the headline.

Overlap the back $\frac{3}{4}$ in. and join the back seam strongly. Wire the headline with support wire. Smooth side of the espartra is placed next the head.

Wire and mull the top of the sideband, or mull only if desired. You now have a cylinder. The part above the head wire will be the sideband, the part below will be stretched to form a little brim. Damp this latter part, being careful not to let the muslin separate from the espartra and avoiding damping the head wire. Work quickly, and stretch the espartra to the desired shape. Use a piece of support wire and fold the raw edge over it; pin through the double espartra close to the wire so that the wire cannot slip. Where the brim is required to stand out, stretch the espartra on to the wire. Allow not less than $1\frac{3}{4}$ in. overlap to the wire and cut it off with the nippers. Fix the wire by wirestitch as described for brim making (page 18), but working through both folds of espartra. Work very tightly and quickly so that it is finished before it is dry, or the pins will rust in. Mould the brim with a hot iron. Trim away the turning closely at the edge of the brim. It is not usually necessary to mull the edge of the brim, as the wire is enclosed in soft esparta. (See illustration in Supplement.)

2. WITH A DOUBLE ESPARTRA BRIM AND NO WIRE AT THE OUTER EDGE. Do not attempt to make a brim wider than 2 in. by this method. Length. Cut the crossway strip equal to head measure plus $1\frac{1}{4}$ in. as above.

Width = sideband plus twice the width of brim and 2 in. turnings. Wire the headline and prepare the sideband as above. Damp the brim part, stretch it well, and fold the raw edge up on to the head wire. The width of the brim is regulated as required. Keep the four-quarter marks of the brim on the quarter marks of the sideband and ease in the extra fullness at the headline. Keep the raw edge in position by back-stitching just above the headline. Trim off the raw edges. Iron the edge of the brim to the required shape with a very hot iron. This may be done on the edge of the table (Supplement) or over the pad, or on a sleeve board.

CHAPTER IV

COVERING SHAPES

MATERIALS should be chosen first of all for lightness, for a heavy hat is an abomination. Materials must also have sufficient substance to avoid allowing stitches and turnings to show through from the foundation. Thin materials must, therefore, have an interlining. The interlining may be either basted to the outer material and treated as one material or may be lightly tacked to the shape with silk or thin cotton. The latter method has the advantage that the turnings are less bulky, because raw edges can be left when the interlining is tacked on and there need be no overlap.

Typical Materials.

Satin. Especially Windsor or Duchess. Silk crêpes and crêpe de Chine, the latter interlined with domette or butter muslin. Taffeta.

Double georgette with an interlining of coloured mercerized lawn. Millinery velvet or plush. Straw cloth. Duvetyne.

For inexpensive coverings, cotton voile over lawn is good. Rough spun silk is effective, and also poplin if light in weight.

Toques, such as described in Chapter III, pages 23, 24, may be covered with some thin material and pads of feathers or flowers. Other materials will come and go with fashion, but the heavier types should be used in a tailored manner. Velveteen and corduroy should be reserved for stitched hats, for example. Further notes on materials will be found in Chapter I.

To gauge quantities. Ascertain the width of the material. Millinery materials range from 12 in. or 14 in. to 18 in. or 27 in. wide. Measure off a portion of the table to the width and lay the paper pattern on the table as if cutting out.

To cut, place the pattern as shown on page 28. Be careful to reverse the brim pattern and cut it once right side *up* and once right side *down*, so that both the brim covering and the underbrim are right side out. Turnings are shown on the diagram. Follow the rule of placing the centre-front to the cross.

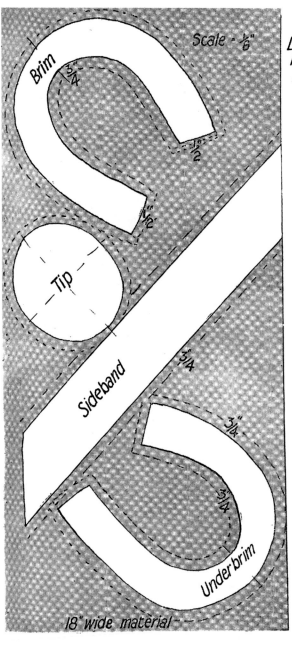

Scale - ⅛"

Brim

¾

½"

½

Tip

Sideband

¾"

¾"

¾"

Under brim

18" wide material

Lay of pattern on
1¼ yards of 18"
Material.

Turnings allowed –
Head   ¾"
Back seam ½"
Elsewhere ¾"

No turnings on
seam of sideband

Covering the Upperbrim.

Mark the headline on the material by tacking and test it with a tape measure (see Chapter III, page 16). Join the back seam of the brim and underbrim in a single seam by means of back-stitching or machine. Use strong sewing silk or button-hole twist, and let the stitches be $\frac{1}{2}$ in. long and quite even. Press the seam open, holding the wrong side over a warm iron. If quite sure that the head-size is correct, snip the turnings with the points of the scissors as far as the head-line, every $\frac{1}{2}$ in. If the snips are farther apart the cover will set badly. Slip the cover over the brim and stab with pins round the headline. Stretch the brim cover over the outer edge with the pins stabbed through the cover and the brim. Fix the four quarters first and then the portions in between. Stitch the cover to the shape by back-stitching just above the head wire, the long stitches on the outside. Turn the outer edge of the cover over to the underbrim, stretching in the same direction as the threads of the material to remove any fullness. Then with the underbrim uppermost, trim off the turnings of the covering to slightly more than the width of the mull, a little at a time, and fix the cover to the mull by hemming, being careful that the hemming stitches do not come to the edge of the brim. If the material is bulky, press lightly. (See illustration in Supplement.)

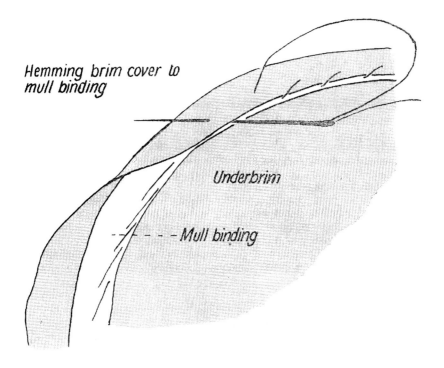

Hemming brim cover to
mull binding

Underbrim

- - - - -Mull binding

Covering the Underbrim with a Piped Edge.

Pin up the back seam, fit, stitch, and press.

Join up a ring of support wire to be equal to a measurement taken just inside the outer edge of the brim. Allow $1\frac{1}{2}$ in. overlap. Bind the join carefully and tightly to cover the sharp ends, and tie with a reef knot so that the wire cannot slip. A damp cotton slips less during binding. Fix the wire on the underbrim with temporary ties about every 4 in.

Lay the underbrim in position on the shape. Note that the four quarters are correct, and stab here and there on the outer edge with pins. Always draw into position in the same direction as the straight thread. Trim the turnings at the outer edge a little way at a time, and use the eye of a large needle to tuck the material between the wire and the edge of the hat. Pin close to the wire through the mull but not through the upper covering.

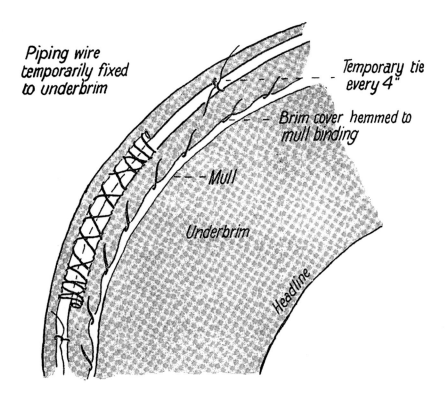

Piping wire temporarily fixed to underbrim

Temporary tie every 4"

Brim cover hemmed to mull binding

Mull

Underbrim

Headline

To Fix the Piped Edge.

Use button-hole twist. Make a knot $1\frac{1}{2}$ in. from the end. Pass the needle
from between the two brims to the right side of the underbrim. *Take a stitch
$\frac{1}{2}$ in. long along under the wire piping and stab through between the two brims.
Hold the cotton tight with the left hand. Pick up a very small stitch on the mull,
pull the cotton through and hold it tight again, pass the needle back through
almost the same hole to come out below the wire on the underbrim. Repeat
from *. The directions are somewhat complicated, but it will be seen from the
illustration that the effect of piping cord is obtained by the long even stitch
lying close up under the wire. At first the cotton may catch on the pins, but
these are removed as the work proceeds.

When a new thread is required, leave an end between the two brims.
Make a milliner's knot on the new thread, take a small stitch on the mull between
the brims; tie the new and the old ends of thread, together with a reef knot;
leave them about 1 in. long, tuck them between the brims, and continue working. Unless the cotton is held very tightly all the time the stitch will slacken
and the join will show. At the end, tie the thread to the beginning thread and
tuck the two ends in.

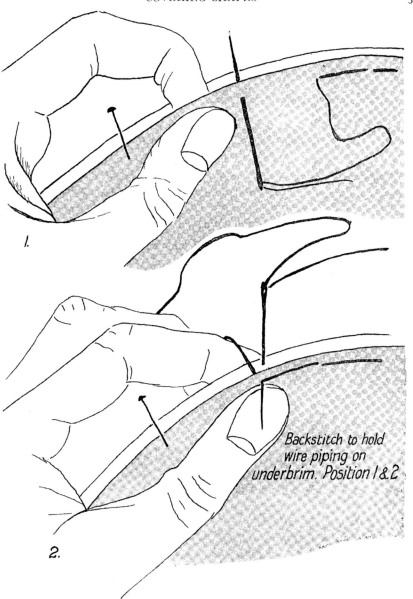

1.

2.

*Backstitch to hold
wire piping on
underbrim. Position 1 & 2*

A Plain Covering may be arranged with the two-edges slip-stitched together instead of piped as above, and this method is suitable for pile fabrics such as velvet, and for straw fabrics with a rib. Coverings may also be arranged with the raw edges of coverings and shape overcast together at the outer edge, and the edge neatened by means of a bind, as for straw hats. (See Chapter VII, page 57.)

To fix the underbrim at the headline. Back stitch the covering $\frac{1}{4}$ in. above the headline, and afterwards snip the turnings every $\frac{1}{2}$ in. The long stitches are on the inside of the crown, and must be placed above the headline to be hidden by the headlining and to avoid the latter showing when the hat is worn.

To Cover a Narrow Brim with Crossway Material.

This is a quick and convenient method which can only be used for brims 2 in. wide or less, or for toques and roll-up brims where the measurement round the outer edge of the brim is not much greater than the head size. There is a limit to the amount which a crossway strip will stretch, so that if the brim were too wide or if the material were rather wiry there would be fullness at the headline, which looks amateurish.

Cut the covering on the direct cross, avoiding more than one join if possible. The upper and the underbrim are covered in one piece.

The length of the strip is equal to the circumference of the brim edge plus $\frac{1}{2}$ in.

The width of the strip is equal to twice the width of the brim, plus $1\frac{1}{2}$ in. turnings, plus a good allowance for loss of width.

It is impossible to give the exact quantity, as materials vary greatly in the amount which they will stretch. Join the strip to form a circle and to fit the outer edge of the brim as tightly as possible, but without bending the brim. Press the seam over an iron; find the half and quarters. Slip the covering over the edge of the brim. Pin through the edge of the brim and arrange the upper brim covering in position at the headline. Back-stitch at the headline just above the line. Avoid any pleats or gathers. Arrange the underbrim in the same way and back-stitch $\frac{1}{4}$ in. above the headline.

If thin material is used, interline it with butter muslin or domette. Cut this to the same size as the material, baste the two together, and treat the two materials as one, simply trimming the interlining away to nothing at the turnings.

Covering Crowns.

Plain Method suitable for crowns of espartra or buckram, and firm blocked net or book muslin. Note that for a net or book muslin crown it is difficult to stick to the inside of the crown the square used with a headlining drawn up with a string, and therefore the square of headlining may be fixed to the inside of the crown by means of long back-stitches before the crown is covered. (Chapter V, page 38, 1.)

Cut the tip covering plus $\frac{1}{2}$ in. turnings. Centre front to the cross, page 27. It is often interlined to give a rich effect. Find the half and quarters. Stretch the covering well over the top. Fix in position by means of back-stitching and stabbing back and forth, and with the long stitches on the outside. Press the turnings lightly to avoid any pucker. The sideband covering is on the cross and needs to fit closely. As it will stretch it may therefore be cut to equal the head measure exactly in length. The width should equal the finished depth plus 2 in. The join should be on the slant and sewn by machine or small even back-stitches exactly on the straight thread. This join should be well pressed over an iron. Turn in the raw edges at top and bottom about $\frac{3}{4}$ in. Note this is less than the 1 in. turning, because stretching the band will reduce the width. Fix

Using a ruler to slip the sideband over the crown.

the turning with a tack. Do not fasten off the tacking but leave an end on the tack thread to allow for stretching. If the material is wiry, hold the band over an upturned iron, press slightly but do not stretch the band. Slip the band over the crown. Use a paper knife or scissors to help, and place the join where it will show least, either at the centre back, or under the trimming. Remove the tacks by cutting the stitches. There is no need for further stitches. For velvet it may be necessary to herringbone or catchstitch the turning of the sideband into position before slipping it over the crown.

PIPED CROWN COVERING suitable for covering a crown made of espartra or buckram. The wire piping is used to emphasize the fashion lines of the crown, and is therefore often used when it is the fashion for crowns to bulge at the top. Cut the tip and sideband as before. Fix the tip in position. Join and press the seam of the sideband, mark the position on the crown for the desired piping. Join up a ring of lappet wire No. 2 or support wire to match the brim piping. Avoid a heavy wire. The ring must fit the desired position exactly and be cut with $1\frac{1}{2}$ in. overlap. For method of joining see page 31. Tie the ring in position with temporary ties of cotton. Turn up the lower edge of the sideband covering and tack. Slip the sideband over the crown, and with a long needle tuck the raw edge between the wire and the crown. Fix with pins as the work proceeds, and cut the temporary ties as needed. Fix piping in the following manner: using buttonhole twist to match, make a millinery knot and bring the needle up from the inside of the crown close under the wire. Take $\frac{3}{4}$ in. back-stitches very close up under the wire. If the thread is pulled tight, the actual stitch will not show but will only throw the wire piping into prominence.

A Soft Draped Crown. This type of crown may be used in conjunction with any type of brim, and need not necessarily have a foundation crown under it. It is suitable for all materials ranging from straw cloth, tulle and net to silk and velvet. It is very becoming, and quick to make, but it takes a good deal of material. The actual width of the sideband depends on folds or tucks. This in turn will depend on the material and whether this is opaque and will hold in position, or transparent and soft, and requires to be caught to a cap headlining or a net foundation. (See Supplement illustration.)

Cut the tip by the pattern either without turnings if a small tip with a roll edge to the crown is required, or with $\frac{1}{2}$ in. turnings if the wearer requires breadth.

Cut the sideband on the cross equal to the head measure in length. The width should be equal to $2\frac{1}{2}$ to 3 times the finished depth. It is usual to interline the material with tarlatan or leno muslin for crêpe de Chine, satin or straw cloth, etc., to make the folds stand well. Baste this to the material and treat as one.

To Join the Tip and Sideband. Join the sideband into a circle to measure 1 in. less than the head measure. (This allows for stretching.) Press the seam over an iron. Find the halves and quarters on both the tip and the sideband. Place the join where it shows least, and turn the sideband wrong side out. Place the right side of the tip to face the right side of the sideband, with the halves and quarters matching. Tack and machine or backstitch the two together. The worker should be very careful to preserve the oval outline of the tip, and may find it a help to chalk a stitching line from the paper pattern. Hold the tip next to the worker while stitching. Trim the turnings. The seam round the tip is sometimes left unpressed, and sometimes the crown is placed wrong side out on the block and the seam flattened open with a warm iron.

Turn up $\frac{3}{4}$ in. at the lower edge, and pin from the right side. Slip over the headband. Fix by slip stitching from the right side. Drape down the extra height in either 2 or 3 folds. These should stand up, and are more becoming if they follow the tilt of the brim, i.e. rise to the left or at the back. For a flat "sailor," follow the lines in fashion and tilt the crown up or down at front or back. Never have the folds quite even. Pin lightly in position from the right side and try on. Catch the folds in position on the wrong side in about eight or ten places. Unless there is a foundation crown, a cap headlining should be inserted to prevent the wearer's head thrusting the folds out of place.

This method may be used without a brim to form a toque for an elder person. In this case it should be mounted on a small headband.

CHAPTER V

HEADLININGS

THE primary use of a headlining is to neaten the inside of the hat. It may further help to strengthen the headline by being made up over a piece of espartra, petersham, or string used as a piping. It will prevent the rough pieces inside the hat pressing on the head of the wearer, as in the case of coarse straw. The lining may take the form of a semi-fitting cap, to which folds and drapery may be caught to prevent their getting disarranged when the head is pushed hurriedly into the hat. A slippery headlining prevents the hair being disarranged.

The material chosen should always be soft and light in weight, but should be crisp enough to fold easily. Taffeta, both real and artificial, and sarcenet are the most suitable materials. Jap silk is good, but is too springy, and the range of suitable colours in this material is limited. Taffeta can generally be obtained in a two-colour shot effect, which will not mark so easily as the plain material. Avoid materials that are "springy."

Mull, muslin, and sateen may be used for hat linings in washing hats, but should be shrunk before being used.

Polanaise is much used for sports hats, and where something really hard wearing is needed. It is useful to prevent the danger of hair slides or knots of hair showing through a soft crown, but is difficult to handle and frays easily.

The lining of a hat should be chosen either to match the hat, or of neutral colour, or to tone with the wearer's hair.

1. Headlining Pulled Up with a Drawstring.

Cut the piece of material on the direct cross. The head measure in length, the width equal to the depth of sideband plus 3 in.

Directions for cutting on the cross will be found in Chapter VII, page 57.

The tip is a 4 in. or 6 in. square of material, and follows the usual rule of centre-front to the cross-thread.

A lining can be obtained from $\frac{3}{8}$ yd. of material, but two joins will be needed. It is more economical to buy a yard and cut it up into as many linings as it will make.

The tip must first be fixed in position. Use a little rubber solution or photo paste at the four corners, or stitch with a few large back-stitches, which must not be visible from the right side. In a covered hat made on a foundation, the tip must be stitched in position before the hat is covered.

Pleat a $\frac{1}{4}$ in. hem on one long side of the sideband. Fix by running. Turn in $\frac{1}{2}$ in. turning at one short end. Press. Place the right side of the lining to the underside of the brim, the join to come equally across the centre back. Allow

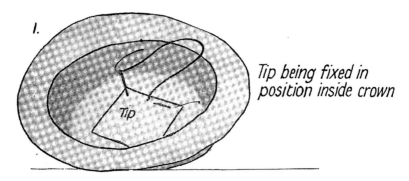

1.

Tip being fixed in position inside crown

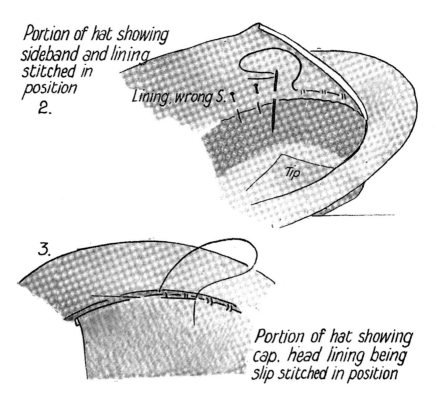

Portion of hat showing sideband and lining stitched in position
2.

Lining, wrong S.

Tip

3.

Portion of hat showing cap. head lining being slip stitched in position

¾ in. to 1 in. turning at the headline. Pin in position with pins at right-angles to the headline. Fix with small stitches ¾ in. apart, which must not show on the outside of the hat. (See illustration, page 38.)

The ¾ in. space between these stitches must form a straight line round the inside of the hat. This line of stitches must be so placed that when the lining is turned into its permanent position inside the hat, no foundation will show. No lining must show when the hat is on the wearer.

Pin the narrow hems together at the top. Overlay the lining for ½ in. at the join, and trim off any surplus material up this seam. Slipstitch up the seam, and finish off. Complete by threading a piece of china ribbon through the hem.

No eyelet holes are required. The bodkin is simply pierced through the hem. Draw up this string.

2. A Closed or Cap Headlining.

May be used in soft hats and draped crowns. Cut the sideband to the same size as the previous lining. The tip is round or oval cut from a 4 in. square of material. Join the sideband with a single seam. Press open. Mark the half and quarters on both tip and sideband.

Turn down the raw edge ¼ in. along one edge and run a gathering thread in, as shown in the illustration. The band is then pulled up to fit the tip, pinned together at the half and quarters and fixed by back-stitching, the stitches being sunk in the gathers.

The lining is then dropped in to the hat, pinned at centre back and centre front. Turn in the raw edges till the lining is the right depth and fix with slip stitching, as shown on page 38, diagram 3.

If extra strength is needed at the headline, a piping cord of thin string may be used as the wire piping in Chapter IV. The sideband may, if preferred, be pleated into the tip instead of gathered. Page 40, diagram 3. If preferred the tip can be larger, using the block as a pattern, and the sideband put flat on to it. This method uses more material, but is flatter and therefore more suitable for Polanaise and crowns made of thick material.

For method of joining see Chapter IV, page 36.

A SPORTS HEADLINING. This is used when it is desirable to line the hat only part of the way up the crown, and a lining and strengthening piece in one can be used. It is a suitable method for felts or for the smoother types of straws.

A piece of espartra, canvas or double leno, cut on the cross, the length of the head measure and 2 in. wide is needed, as well as the headlining and a length of china ribbon. Cut the lining on the cross. The length equals head measure plus ½ in. for join. The depth equals the finished width plus 2½ in.

Join this strip into a circle to fit the inside of the crown, and press the turnings open. Run a ¼ in. hem along one edge. Tack the strengthening piece 2 in. in from the raw edge overlapping for the join at the back, turn the raw edge up to enclose the strengthening piece, and machine through the three thicknesses in some decorative manner, as shown on page 41, diagram 2.

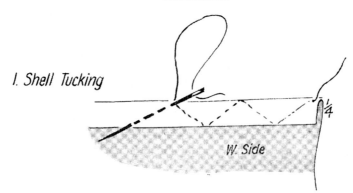

1. Shell Tucking

¼

W. Side

2. Sideband, neatened by
   Shell running, being
   fixed to oval tip.

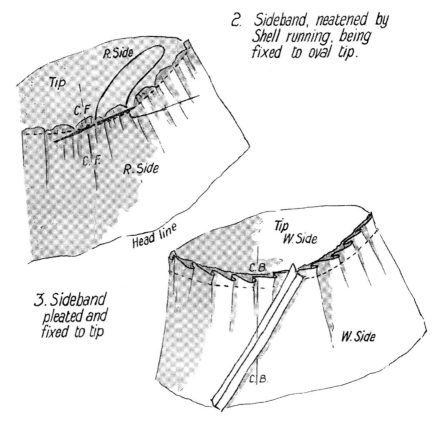

R. Side

Tip

C. F

C. F   R. Side

Head line

Tip
W. Side

C. B.

3. Sideband
   pleated and
   fixed to tip

W. Side

C. B.

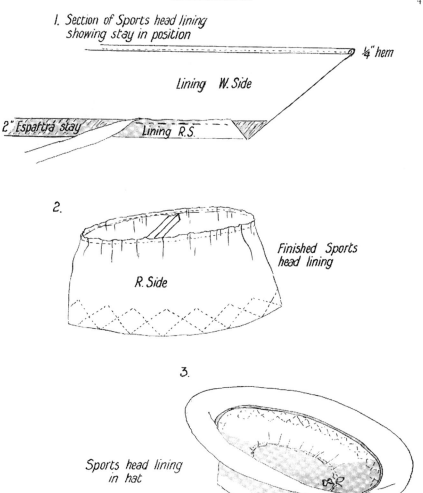

1. Section of Sports head lining showing stay in position

¼" hem

Lining   W. Side

2" Espartra stay

Lining   R.S.

2.

Finished Sports head lining

R. Side

3.

Sports head lining in hat

Run a length of china ribbon through the small hem at the top of the lining. Insert the lining in the same way as shown for the cap headlining.

These linings can be modified to suit the different styles of hats. An espartra stay can be put in a cap headlining and stitched in the same way as a sports headlining, making a firm foundation to which to catch any folds. This is useful in soft straw hats that are not wired at the head and tend to get out of shape.

CHAPTER VI

FELT HATS

OWING to the present-day vogue for short hair and hats that are soft and comfortable to wear, felt hats remain in fashion all the year round.

There is an almost endless choice of shade and colour in felt hoods, and no headfitting need be considered when buying them. Colour and quality only have to be considered. For this reason it is so satisfactory to make one's own hats.

What is still more interesting is to have one's own individual hat, and not one of a type that has been made in a factory by the hundred.

For sports and everyday wear the hat may be made up quite simply, while for more formal occasions it may be made up with folds, tucks, pleats, incrustations of some contrasting material, or reverse sections of its own material.

Felt hats can be made with the brim in one with the crown or with the brim made separately from the crown and joined later.

Treatment of Different Kinds of Felts.

Felt is obtained in hoods. The cheaper makes are smaller and do not give much scope for fancy effects.[1]

Some of the other kinds of felt need slightly different treatment. A good plan is to take a strip of felt from the edge of the brim and notice its reaction to water and heat.

ANGORA FELTS are very delicate when wet, and need most careful handling. All manipulation must be carried out with the palms of the hands, as the fingers will poke through easily. They tear, if pulled too hard. Always brush up after blocking with a soft, not a stiff brush, and work with the pile, which is very marked in this type of felt.

Felts with a Glossy Finish.

As this gloss is obtained by ironing down the pile of the felt during making, it is lost as soon as the pile is disturbed by water, or the steam from a kettle.

After blocking, iron the hat very evenly all over, working with the pile and holding a piece of muslin between the felt and the iron.

Glycerine or methylated spirits can then be rubbed gently into the felt, always working with the pile, and using a very small quantity of glycerine or methylated spirit at a time. Polish by brushing with the pile, using a soft brush.

---

[1] Wool felts are the cheapest kind and wear fairly well. They are suitable for beginners to work on. They spot with the rain. Fur felts are better quality, easier to manipulate. wear best, and are obtainable in a greater variety of colours.

Velours.

Are blocked in the same way as wool or fur felts, but must be brushed hard with a wire brush to restore their fluffy look.

Before starting to make the hat the worker must provide herself with a block, to her own head measure. (See Chapter I, page 1).

A hood, with buttonhole twist, or strong cotton (not Sylko) to match it exactly.

Millinery needles, size 5. Large pins. ¾ yd. petersham ribbon 1¼ in. wide to strengthen the headline.

Scissors, and a knife or razor blade.

Some flannel to be used when pressing the hat, as the iron marks the felt easily.

An illustration of the hat to be made, and the measurements that will be used in the making. Directions for taking these measurements will be found in Chapter I, page 7. They should be : size of head, length centre back to centre front of crown, side-to-side measure, and the width of the brim at the front, back, and sides.

A bowl of hot water. As the colour may run it is necessary to set it. For light colours dissolve one tablespoonful of salt in the hot water. For dark colours use a tablespoonful of vinegar. An iron, and an ironing blanket.

A brim pattern, prepared according to the directions in Chapter II, page 8.

Everything must be prepared beforehand, as it is imperative to work quickly. While the felt is wet and hot it is very easy to manipulate. Directly it gets cold it hardens, and is nearly impossible to work.

To Make the Crown.

Put the hood into the basin of hot water. Remove, and do not let the water run out through the top of the crown, or it will stretch the felt ; a fault that is difficult to rectify later on. Work the crown down into position using the palm of the hands, because the felt is tender when wet and it is easy to poke fingers through it.

Tie a string tightly round at the headline.

Extra fullness can be shrunk away with the iron. Cover the crown with flannel, and press with the heel of the iron.

Cut the brim off just below the string, using the knife or razor blade.

Mark the centre-back and centre-front of the crown with tailors chalk, or a tack. Put the block in a warm place to dry.

To Make the Brim.

Take the remaining piece of felt. Choose the best side for the centre-front. Cut through the centre-back to allow it to lie flat on the table.

Arrange the previously prepared brim pattern on this felt. The only turning required is ¾ in. at the headline.

If the felt is not the right size, re-damp it in hot water, and it will then be found quite possible to manipulate it to the shape required, but work quickly before the felt hardens. If necessary, extra fullness can be shrunk away with the iron. To do this put the brim on the ironing blanket, wrong side up, and cover with a piece of dry flannel. Use the iron fairly hot and press, using a circular movement. Try the pattern frequently to avoid shrinking the felt too much.

When the right size is obtained, and the brim is quite dry, pin the pattern in position. Tack round the headline.

Tack, or mark with tailors chalk, the outer edge and the back join. Mark the centre-front with a tack.

Take away the pattern and test the headline. This must be exact.

Cut off the extra material at the outer edges and the back, leaving no turnings. Use a ruler to straighten the back seam. Leave $\frac{3}{4}$ in. turnings at headline, to join crown and brim later on.

To Join the Centre-back of the Brim.

One of two methods may be used.

By OVERSEWING worked on the underside of the brim and with the stitches loose enough to allow the join to lie flat when complete.

By A FLAT JOIN. Use buttonhole twist to exactly match the straw and a millinery needle.

Tie a millinery knot at the end of the twist. Hold the two edges to be joined together and start working from the headline.

Make a slanting stitch between the two thicknesses of felt from about $\frac{1}{8}$ in. in from the join on one side to $\frac{1}{4}$ in. beyond the join on the other side.

The needle must pass in the thickness of the felt and show neither on right or wrong side.

Insert the needle at almost the same point as it comes out.

Continue working till the edge of the brim is reached, then work back to the headline and tie to the end left at the beginning.

Press. Test the headline.

Snip the turnings at the headline, every $\frac{3}{4}$ in. to allow them to lie flat inside the crown of the hat.

Make up the piece of petersham into a band to fit the head exactly. Mark the centre-front and centre-back.

Pin the brim on to this band, centre-front and backs matching, and the snipped turnings on the outside. Tack and try on.

Stitch the brim to the petersham band, catching in the points, as shown in Chapter III, page 19.

To Join the Brim and Crown.

When the crown is absolutely dry take it off the block. If this is done while the crown is still damp it will stretch at the headline.

Place the crown over the brim and petersham band, centre-fronts and centre-back matching. Pin by stabbing the pins into the felt. Tack and try on. Any alterations in the depth of the crown must be made at this point.

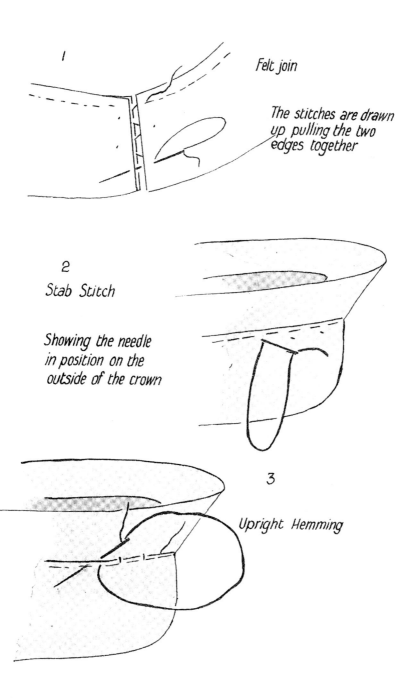

1

Felt join

The stitches are drawn up pulling the two edges together

2

Stab Stitch

Showing the needle in position on the outside of the crown

3

Upright Hemming

Stab Stitch.

Fix by stab stitch shown in the illustration on page 45. Start with a millinery knot and stab the needle in from the wrong side. Re-insert the needle into the same hole but sloping from right to left. Make the stitches about $\frac{1}{2}$ in. apart.

Hemming.

If preferred, the crown can be hemmed to the brim. The stitches are worked in at the brim and out on the crown, the hat being held with the crown towards the worker and the brim upwards. The stitches should be about $\frac{1}{8}$ in. in depth and $\frac{1}{4}$ in. apart.

Put the hat carefully on the block with the centre-front to the centre of the block.

Cover with a piece of flannel and press round the headline, keeping the heel of the iron parallel with the brim.

Press the brim if necessary, supporting the crown on the hand, while the brim lies flat on the table.

If the hat has been marked with the iron the mark can be removed by first holding it in the steam from a kettle, which should be so directed that it comes through from the wrong to the right side. Then by brushing with a small stiff brush, brushing with the pile. Use a wire brush for velours. If liked the hat can now be stiffened on the inside of the crown and the underside of the brim, using one of the preparations sold for this purpose by any millinery store or warehouse.

Trim the hat.

Insert a headlining, if the petersham band is not thought sufficient, and the hat is then complete.

More Advanced Methods

To Insert Pieces of Felt into a Crown or Brim.

These pieces may be inserted in the crown only or continued from the crown on to the brim. They may be the same felt as the hat, wrong side out, to give an effect of light and shade, or of some other felt. When blocking the crown draw the position of the pieces on the crown with tailor's chalk or mark the outline on the damp felt with scissors. When the felt is dry use the knife and cut out the piece while the hat is on the block. This will leave a hole, and the piece cut out may be turned wrong side out and used to form an insertion if it is a square, diamond, oval, round, etc., but if the piece cut out is a different shape on two sides, a new piece must be cut from the pieces left over or some other hood. Use the cut out piece as a pattern and use the razor blade to cut the new piece on the board.

To Fix the Insertion in Position.

Tie-tack the corners first and then use the same stitch as used for the felt join (page 45) or any fancy embroidery stitch used for joining edges. Press the work well under the damp flannel on the block and brush the seams while the steam rises.

Felt and straw may be joined in the same way. The difficulty to be dealt with being that the straw may fray; the edge of the straw must be turned in or otherwise neatened before joining to the felt.

Tucks in a Felt Hat.

These are mostly used for decorations. They should be made before the hood is blocked. Mark the position with chalk or tack. Bear in mind that the tucks must form a becoming line to the wearer, and that they must be really well made and quite even. Use buttonhole twist to match the hood or strong cotton. A piece of fine soft string is sometimes a help. Place the string on the wrong side of the tuck line. Pinch up the tuck to enclose the string and prick stitch backwards and forwards below the string. The stitches should be close together and tight, and the fastening on and off firm. When the tucks are finished, steam them well from the wrong side. Place the hood on the block and press and brush as usual.

Tucks on a Brim.

These show the wrong side, and it is difficult to conceal the string, so it is better omitted. Pull the stitching very tight or the thread will show on the wrong side. (See illustrations in Supplement.)

Pleats and Folds.

These may be arranged on crown and brim while the hood is wet. It may be necessary to tack them into position when making them and iron them lightly under a damp flannel. Use silk or Sylko for tacking, as it will mark less.

To Make a Folded Felt Hat with Crown and Brim in One Piece.

Choose a soft felt hood. Take very careful measurements from front to back and side to side. Dip the hood in hot water as described above. Place on the block and fix a string at headline. Check up the front to back and side-to-side measures carefully and adjust the string if required. Work quickly. This type of hat will usually be made with the brim folded close to the crown at one part either from front to back on the left or across the front or the back. Turn this part of the brim close up to the crown at the headline and press the headline firmly with a hot iron, covering the part to be pressed with a damp flannel or net. It will be found that the part of the brim still to be dealt with is too full; therefore cut this part of the brim partly away from the crown. Cut the brim just below the string and across the width of the brim in one piece. The position of the cut across the brim is determined by the style (see Supplement). It depends on whether the ends of felt are used as part of the trimming and finished in a knot or drapery, or whether a portion has to be cut off and an ordinary brim join is to be made (see page 45).

(*a*) If the hat is to have a seam in the brim, while still damp, gently stretch the part of the brim which was touching the crown until it becomes less circular. Fit to the crown size. Cut off the surplus amount, putting the join at the most inconspicuous place. Join and press the brim. Lap the detached part of the brim under the crown for $\frac{1}{2}$ in. running off to nothing where it is joined to the crown. Rejoin the crown to the brim by upright hemming. (See page 45.)

(*b*) With the ends of the brim forming a tie or bow, slant the cut through the brim as for the ends of ribbon. Stretch the cut ends to make them less circular. Lap the detached part over the crown and hem it to the crown. Fix the ends in any way that suits the wearer. The whole thing must be worked swiftly and lightly or the felt will thicken. The hat should be strengthened at the headline as directed on page 44, and finished with any desired trimming and a headlining. After which it should be placed on the block and lightly finished off with a hot iron used over a damp cloth, and brush the hat well to make the pile lie in one direction. If possible, allow the hat to stiffen and cool before removing from the block.

CHAPTER VII

STRAWS

CURIOUS as it may sound, few straw hats worn by present-day women are actually made of straw. This is owing to the advent of the modern threshing machine. A few straws are made by hand in Buckinghamshire, and some are imported from Japan and elsewhere abroad. Substitutes of every sort are employed, and therein lie pitfalls for the unwary.

To assist the worker as much as possible, the Supplement contains a list of so-called straws with notes on their treatment. In any case it is wise to snip off a scrap of whatever is to be used and make a few experiments before beginning work. Fashion is continually inventing new materials and it is well-nigh impossible to give directions for all types.

This chapter gives directions for making up straws under the following headings—

1. Straw plait bought in bundles or by the yard.
    (a) With crown and brim in one piece, beginning from the centre of the tip.
    (b) With crown and brim separately, beginning the crown from the centre and the brim from the outer edge.
2. Blocking straw hoods.
    (a) Crown and brim separately, the edge of brim neatened by
        (i) Stretched petersham.
        (ii) Wired and bound with ribbon.
        (iii) Crossway binding.
    (b) Crown and brim in one piece.
3. To varnish straws.

1. WHEN MAKING HATS OF STRAW PLAIT

It will be found that the coarser straws are easier to handle.

The amount of straw required to make a hat of this type varies with the width of straw chosen and size of the hat. For a garden hat, with a 22 in. to 23 in. head measure and a 2 in. to 3 in. brim, 12–14 yd. of straw 1 in. to $1\frac{1}{4}$ in. wide will be ample.

Prepare as for the felt hat, Chapter VI. Besides this apparatus the worker must provide herself with the straw chosen. Strong cotton or buttonhole twist to match it. A pattern for the tip, directions for which will be found in Chapter II, pages 9 and 10.

Start making the hat at the centre of the crown, and work down to the edge of the brim.

The Tip.

To start, dip the end of the straw in water. Twist it, and bind with cotton. (See diagram page 51.)

The amount of moisture necessary varies with the different types of straw. The table on pages 91–95 will assist the worker to form her own judgment.

Always work from right to left. Begin to form a circle, and sew it in position. After the first row is complete, manipulate the straw so that the first row overlaps the succeeding row $\frac{1}{3}$ its width. Ease to allow the straw to lie flat.

Damp the straw on the back or wrong side as often as necessary during work.

A frequent fault occurs here. The worker tends to ease too much and the outer edge becomes fluted; or holds the straw too closely with the result that the circle will not lie flat.

To avoid these faults, pin a complete circle of straw in position and test it by laying it flat on the table before stitching. Straw being woven diagonally is elastic, and will stretch or ease in the same way as material cut on the cross.

If an oval crown is required, work until the circle measures about 3 in. across. Mark the centre-back and centre-front with ties of cotton, then overlap the straw slightly more than $\frac{1}{3}$ its width at the sides.

The stitch used to sew the straw together must be sunk into the plait, both to avoid the cotton showing and to prevent the straw splitting.

The stitch is stabbed into the straw from the right to the wrong side. (See page 51.)

Continue working until the tip is the same size as the pattern and lies quite flat.

Leave the plait hanging and press on the wrong side, over a soft pad, under a cloth, using a cool iron.

Straw hats

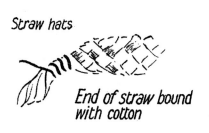

End of straw bound
with cotton

Beginning of straw tip

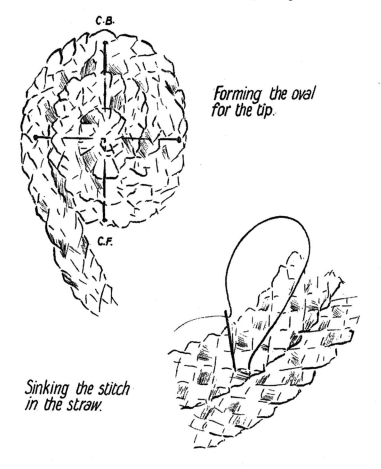

Forming the oval
for the tip.

Sinking the stitch
in the straw.

The Sideband.

Re-mark the centre-back and centre-front. Start the sideband about 2 in. before the centre-back is reached.

Slope very gradually and cease easing the straw. (See page 53.)

The first row, which will take all the strain of the curve, must be sewn very firmly and evenly.

Continue to work down the side of the crown underlapping the straw $\frac{1}{3}$ its width. Test the head size frequently, as it is very easy for an inexperienced worker to pull the crown in to a small size.

The easiest method of making the crown even is to mark the centre-back very definitely.

Measure off a length of straw, the size of the head measure, marking with a pin, but leaving the plait hanging.

Arrange this length in position, pinned all round, before starting to sew.

Continue till the crown is the right depth, then start the brim, which can be made all in one with the crown or separately and joined to the crown afterwards.

The Brim.

For a simple hat, with not much variation in the width of the brim, the brim and crown may be made in one. For a larger and more shaped brim it will be necessary to cut a brim pattern in strong paper. (See Chapter II, page 6.) Work from the directions in the latter part of this chapter.

The Brim in One with the Crown.

Start to shape the brim about 2 in. before the centre-back. (See page 53.)

Ease the straw on to the lower edge of the crown and sew very securely. This easing is done with the thumb and finger of the left hand, and must be very even and sufficient to make the brim stand out at right angles from the crown, keeping the straw underlapped $\frac{1}{3}$ of its width and the stitches close.

The stitch must now be hidden on both upper and underside of the straw, and the long stitch lying between the two thicknesses of straw plait.

Continue working the brim. In the case of a flat brim (a sailor type of hat) the straw must be eased sufficiently to allow the brim to lie almost flat on the table but must not be "frilly." If a mushroom or a turn-up shape is needed, the straw is eased less. This will give the turned up or down effect.

The width of the brim must now be considered. If a brim the same width all round is needed, continue to work until this width is obtained.

Keep the stitches hidden on both the upper and the underside of the brim. When the correct width is obtained, cut off the remaining straw at the back, leaving about 2 in. hanging, which must be gradually worked in under the edge of the brim.

If the brim is to be shaped narrower at the back and front, overlap the straw at these places in the same way as when making the oval tip.

If a wire is needed at the outer edge put it on at this stage.

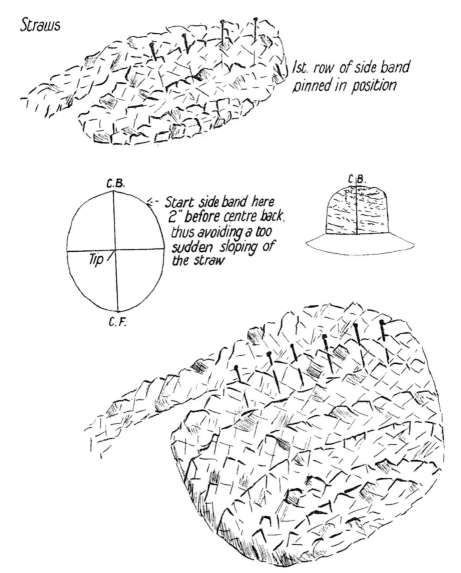

Straws

1st. row of side band
pinned in position

C.B.

Tip

C.F.

Start side band here
2" before centre back,
thus avoiding a too
sudden sloping of
the straw

C.B.

To Wire the Edge.

Take a measure $\frac{1}{4}$ in. inside the circumference of the brim. Cut off a length of millinery wire equal to the above measure plus $1\frac{1}{2}$ in. for join. Join into a circle, see Chapter IV, page 31, and fix $\frac{1}{4}$ in. in from the edge of the brim on the underside, using wire stitch, the directions for which will be found in Chapter III, page 17.

This wire must now be covered. Use a piece of straw sewn to the under edge of the brim, the outer edges even, and only sewn in position along the outer edge. This piece of straw should be joined in a circle before being sewn to the hat, and the method used for joining is that always employed for any joins in coarse straw. Unplait about $1\frac{1}{2}$ in. of both ends of the straw, having first damped them. Then re-plait the two ends together, using a coarse needle, which should be woven through the straw before it is threaded. Neaten all the loose ends of straw by darning them in, working from both sides. Press the join, on the wrong side, under a damp cloth before fixing the circle to the hat.

The brim should now be pressed. Hold it wrong side up, flat on the table over a soft ironing pad, as illustrated in the supplement, and press under a damp cloth. It is a great improvement if the hat is now put on the block and the crown pressed all over under a thick, damp cloth.

To strengthen and soften the headline. This can be accomplished in various ways. A piece of petersham the head measure plus $1\frac{1}{2}$ in. for the join and $1\frac{1}{4}$ in. to 2 in. wide, can be joined into a circle and sewn above the headline inside the crown and no further lining used. The drawback to this method being that the rough straw will catch on the hair.

A better method is to take a crossway strip of espartra the length of the head measure plus $1\frac{1}{2}$ in. for join $\times$ $1\frac{1}{2}$ in. wide. Join this into a circle and mull the edges. Directions for mulling will be found in Chapter III, page 18. Sew this into the hat, $\frac{1}{8}$ in. above the headline, noticing that the stitches do not show on the right side.

Block a piece of net or leno as explained in Chapter III, page 23, using about a 12 in. square. When blocked, trim off all rough edges and put the net crown into the tip of straw hat. This hat crown should not come as far down as the headline, in fact, if it comes halfway down the side of the crown it will be sufficient. It may be stitched in place if liked, using as few stitches as possible along the lower edge, but if it has been well blocked and if the hat is gently pressed on the block with the net inside, stitches should be unnecessary.

The hat is now ready for trimming and lining.

With finer types of straw, Tagel, Dunstable, or a similar kind, it will be found difficult to work the straw in the manner suggested in the previous part of this chapter.

THE CROWN AND BRIM MUST BE MADE SEPARATELY and joined when finished. This method can be used for coarse straws where a large brim is required.

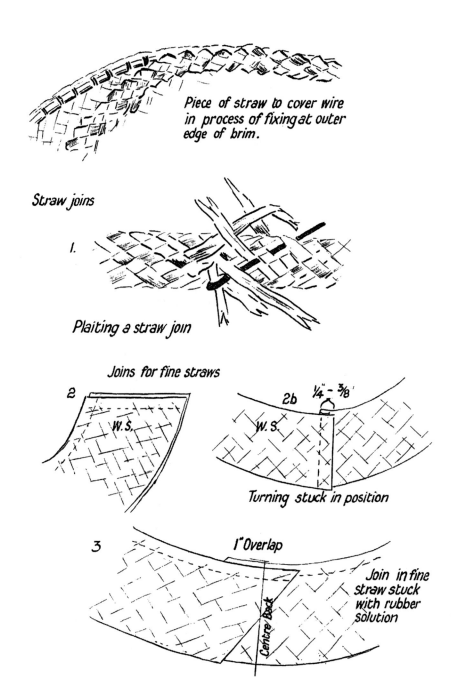

Piece of straw to cover wire in process of fixing at outer edge of brim.

Straw joins

1.

Plaiting a straw join

Joins for fine straws

2

W.S.

2b   ¼" – ⅜"

W.S.

Turning stuck in position

3   1" Overlap

Centre Back

Join in fine straw stuck with rubber solution

To Make the Crown on the Block.

The tip is started in the same way as the tip for coarse straw. (See page 51.) It may be fixed by running on right side (Tagel), machining or hemming (cheap Tagel) on wrong side. When it is 3 in. across put it, wrong side up, on to the block. Fix with a drawing pin in the centre of the crown. Then continue working the straw in position, pinning it to the previous row with the hat still on the block. In this case the last row will always overlap the preceding row for one-third its width. Continue working down the crown till it is the required depth. When at about 2 in. from the centre-back cut off surplus straw. Leave 2 in. end and gradually slant this off over the crown. Mark the centre-back and centre-front. Turn the crown right side out. Prepare a pattern for the brim as explained in Chapter II, and cut this out in stout brown paper, join the pattern up the centre-back. Start working 2 in. from the centre-back, arranging the straw round the extreme outer edge of the pattern, but with the right side of the straw upwards. Fix by running stitch worked from the right side. If hemming is used, tack first, remove the straw from the paper, and hem on the wrong side.

Continue working until the pattern is covered.

With the more shaped brims, spaces will occur where the brim is widest. These must be filled in with short lengths of straw. (See diagram 2, page 57.) But in every case the last row must be a complete circle holding the short ends in position. Add another 1 in. to form a headband to slip inside the crown. Mark the centre-back and centre-front. Remove the pattern. Wire the outer edge of the brim as for a coarse straw, but using lappet wire No. 2 instead of support wire, which is too heavy.

This must be covered by a piece of straw fixed in the same way as for coarse straw, but with a back join instead of plaiting the two ends of straw together.

A crossway bind may be preferred, and is described in this Chapter, page 59.

Or use a binding of ribbon or petersham. Where this is done, press the brim the wrong side, over a soft pad, avoiding the headband which must be left standing and keeping the shape carefully. Put the crown on to the block right side out, press gently under a thick cloth. When quite dry, remove the crown from the block. Strengthen the headline, using one of the methods suggested at the beginning of this Chapter.

To Join the Crown and Brim.

Slip the crown over the brim, centre-fronts and backs matching. Stitch together, using $\frac{1}{2}$ in. back stitch, long stitches on the inside, no stitch showing on the outside.

To Line the Underbrim.

A soft finish to the underbrim is sometimes liked. Tulle or net to match the straw may be used. Six to eight thicknesses of tulle or a double layer of net will be required. If a contrast is preferred, georgette, or chiffon used double, with or without an interlining of lawn, may be employed. This underbrim may be fixed in one of two ways—

Straw Hats

Showing the arrangement of straw
to fill in the spaces at the side of
a large brim.

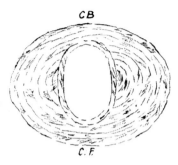

CB

C.F.

Crossway cutting and joining

Cutting the
strip = 6 times the
finished width

R.S   *W.S*

Joining the
crossway strip

The strips joined. Each join
must follow the grain of
the material.

Binding stitched in
position at outer
edge of brim

Wire

¼   Binding

Right side of brim

Under-side of brim
with binding slip-
stitched in position.

As the underbrim described in Chapter IV, page 30, either with or without a piping wire. Or caught to the outer edge of the brim, the raw edges covered by the last piece of straw.

Owing to the elasticity of the materials used for underbrims a back join is rarely needed. Even with a shaped brim the net or tulle can be stretched to the required shape.

2. BLOCKING STRAW HATS

Straw hats are also made from straw bought in hoods similar to felt hoods. Bear in mind that straw hoods are made in many imitations of straw and proceed cautiously. Make the same preparation before blocking as for felt hats. (See Chapter VI, page 43.)

The hood may be either soaked in tepid water for varying lengths of time according to its nature, or held in the steam of a kettle. It is advisable to take a small cutting and test which method is the most suitable for the type of straw in hand. Notes about the different kinds of straw will be found in the supplement. If a dull finished effect is desired and a straw varnish is not to be used, dissolve about 2 tablespoonfuls or more of gum in a pint of warm water. (See page 2 for notes on making gum.)

About 3 measures of powdered gelatine to a pint of water used warm is useful for crochet hats. Do not let the mixture "set" but use it warm.

Sometimes it is a struggle to place the hat on the block. Some straw hoods may be made up of fine plait. There is a chance of splitting the machining. It can, of course, be mended, but there is a danger of the mend showing, and it is therefore better to place the hood on the block before damping and place the whole thing in the water or steam.

Other straws are woven diagonally from the centre of the crown to the edge of the brim, and must be worked firmly on to the block, using the palms of the hands to work the crown down and pulling the brim fairly hard and diagonally working with the thread as it is woven. It is sometimes quite hard work, but patience will accomplish the result.

Should there be fullness, if much, arrange a pleat at a becoming angle as part of the decoration, or if little, endeavour to shrink it away with a cool iron. Remember grass, horsehair, and straw do not shrink, only cotton, wool or kindred materials which may be woven in with straw, therefore most fullness must be removed by hard pulling.

After the crown is blocked and the string tied tightly round at the correct headline, decide if it is possible to keep the brim in one piece with the crown. If possible, do so, as straw frays and it is better to avoid joins either at the headline or at the back seam. When the sideband is too deep for fashion it must be cut.

For a Crown and Brim Separately.

Cut off the brim, leaving 1 in. turning below the string on the crown. After the crown is dry remove from the block. If the edge is to be covered with trimming it may be left raw and cut off at the headline, simply taking care that it does not stretch before it is attached to the headband.

If the lower edge is not to be covered, neaten it by

(a) Binding with ribbon petersham. Join the ribbon into a circle first, press the seam and pin the halves and quarters in position to avoid stretching the crown (for directions see page 76).

(b) Turn up the raw edge on to the inside of the crown while the latter is slightly damp. Press in position while damp. Avoid stretching.

The Brim when Separate from the Crown.

Make a pattern in paper, as described in Chapter II, page 6. If the brim is designed to be nearly flat it may be made without a back seam and a little drawn in at the outer edge of the brim when the latter is wired or bound, etc. Pleats may be ironed in to shape a flat brim and to cause it to droop, but if there is much shaping the brim must have a seam.

Lay the pattern on the brim, outline the head and the outer edge by tacking cotton, mark the centre front. Cut out, leaving

$\frac{3}{4}$ in. turning at the head
$\frac{3}{4}$ in.   ,,   ,,   ,,   outer edge
$\frac{1}{4}$ in. or 1 in. at the join. (See diagram 2, page 55.)

The turning at the outer edge is largely to allow for fraying, therefore it is sometimes possible to manage with a little less.

The back join depends on the type of straw. Refer to the diagram on page 55. Use method two for medium coarse straw and method three for fine straw. Complete this join according to the diagram. Press under a cloth if necessary. Wire the headline if desired with support wire No. 6 (Chapter III, page 16), or join up a strengthening strip and attach it to the head (Chapter III, page 18). Test up the head size frequently.

Treatment of the Outer Edge of the Brim.

(a) TURN IN RAW EDGE WHILE DAMP. Tack and press, machine round once or more with a cotton to match or stab stitch firmly by hand. Either leave as it is or, after the use of stiffening mixture or varnish, neaten the raw edge with a stretched petersham ribbon stuck on with rubber solution. This method is soft and suitable for small sports or tennis hats or for large floppy artistic hats. The petersham is heavy on a wide brim which has not been wired. (For directions see Chapter X, page 76.)

(b) EDGE WIRED AND BOUND. Measure the outer edge of the paper pattern. Cut off a length of lappet wire No. 2 for fine straws—the brim measure plus $1\frac{1}{2}$ in. turnings. Join this in a circle as shown on page 31. Place this circle under the brim, fold the damp edge of straw over the brim so that the wire comes to the tacked outline and wire-stitch through the double straw. Use 50 or 60 cotton and follow directions on page 18. Trim off the raw edge closely.

Neaten this wire by means of a ribbon bind (Chapter X, page 76). A velvet bind, or by crossway binding.

To cut the material on the cross, see diagram on page 57. Special care must be taken in joining the cut pieces, that they all shade the same way, and in the case of ribbed material, that the join is made down the rib.

The binding should be cut six times the required width plus a little for extra loss of width in stretching round the edge of the hat. Therefore a bind to be $\frac{1}{4}$ in. when finished should be $1\frac{3}{4}$ in. wide.

Join into a circle to fit tightly round the edge of the brim. The join must be most carefully made. Pull a thread at the ends of the bind to ensure the join being made on a straight thread, backstitch firmly together, and press the join open with a hot iron. The silk used for sewing the bind must match exactly in colour, and if cotton is used it must be fine, and of the exact colour. The bind must be very carefully measured, as if it is made too tight or too loose it will have a home-made look and spoil the finished effect of the hat. After sewing in a circle fold the bind in halves lengthways, cover with a cloth, and press with an iron. Pin on to the edge of the brim, right side of the bind to the upperside of the brim, raw edges of bind and brim equal. Fix in position with pins stabbed into the bind and the brim to avoid marking the straw and bind. Fix with backstitching, the stitches $\frac{1}{8}$ in. long, the long stitch on the upperside of the brim. Press gently under a damp cloth, being very careful not to mark the bind. Turn the bind over on to the outside of the brim and slip hem in position (see diagram, page 57), using fine silk to exactly match the bind. It will be found very easy to pull the bind over the raw edges and to regulate it so as to avoid lumps. Being cut on the cross it will be elastic and very pliable. Press lightly when completed under a thick cloth and over a soft pad.

To join the hat brim to the crown. Pin together with centre-front and back of crown to centre-front and back of brim, stabbing the pins in and the crown over the brim. Tack and fit on. Make any necessary alterations. Then fix firmly together with backstitch or stab stitch, but in any case the stitch must be firm and invisible from the right side. The stitch should be worked at about $\frac{1}{2}$ in. from the edge, sometimes two rows are advisable, when a bind is used, then the stitch should come just at the place where the bind is fixed on to the crown. Leave an end of silk or cotton hanging inside the hat when starting to sew, to enable the worker to tie off the finished end. Put the hat on to the block and press round the headline.

For Brim and Crown all in One Piece.

This is only possible with a slightly turned down brim and with fairly manageable straws. That is to say, it must be possible to work the type of straw when it is damp as if it were being shrunk. Block the crown. Tie a string at the headline. Tack a mark for the centre-front and back. Continue working while the hood is damp. Pull the brim out sharply from the headline. Decide the shape for the outer edge of the brim and mark with pins. Take a piece of wire and fix it to the edge of the brim by means of wire stitch. A good deal of shaping may be effected while the wire is being fixed on if the worker either eases or stretches the brim on the wire. Further directions for this and for joining the wire will be found in Chapter III, page 18. Trim off the raw edges after wiring. Press the crown on the block with a warm iron, covering the straw with a thick, damp cotton cloth. Allow the hat to dry on the block, then take it off and crease the new headline firmly with the finger and thumb. Place the upperside of the brim right side down on the ironing table. (See illustration, supplement.) Support the crown with the knee and the left hand and press the brim with the heel of the iron. Cover the brim with a slightly damp rag if required. Allow the hat to get quite dry and varnish it if required. See note on varnishes, page 2. Neaten the outer edge in the same way as described above.

To neaten and strengthen the inside of the headline various methods can be employed, and these vary with the different types of straws; some straws are much stiffer than others, and more protection for the head must be provided.

A piece of espartra, mulled at the edge can be used, directions for working will be found in Chapter III, page 18. This will be placed inside the hat $\frac{1}{8}$th from edge of crown, the muslin side to come next to the wearer's head and fixed in position with prick stitch, in the same way as the crown and brim were fixed together. Then insert a headlining, the directions for which will be found in Chapter V, page 39.

Another method is by using a headlining strengthened by espartra or book muslin, directions for making will be found in Chapter V, page 39.

In every case it is as well to put the hat back on to the block and press it before putting in the headlining. When pressing, the heel of the iron should be used along the base of the crown, and a thick cloth should be placed between the iron and the hat.

Hats should always be trimmed before a closed type of head lining is inserted, and this point must be considered when lining a hat.

CHAPTER VIII

MAKING UP SECTIONAL HATS AND CAPS—
STITCHED HATS—BERETS

Making Up Stitched Hats.

1. CHOICE OF PATTERN. If the hats are required for games, travelling, or sports, they must keep on well, and be fairly small.

The brim is not wired, therefore choose a narrow brim to avoid "flopping." Two inches is an average width. Wider than this requires an espartra foundation or it will "flop" like a picture hat. It is often wise to design the brim to roll up or down, as the tightness helps to keep it in position. The brim may stretch a little in working, so design the pattern to roll a little closer than required for the final result.

The crown may be tip and sideband as on page 9, Chapter II, or sectional, as on page 10, Chapter II.

The material is usually interlined to give richness and firmness. At the moment of writing some stitched tweed and linen hats are made without interlining, the raw edge being turned over and stitched and the brim either starched or stiffened as for straw. They do not wear well and are probably a passing fashion.

2. CHOICE OF MATERIAL. As light as possible but firm enough to admit of a tailored finish.

Outer Covering	Interlining for Crown	Stiffening for Brim
Linen	Lawn or mull muslin	Double book muslin, tailors or millinery canvas
Firm cottons	Do.	Do.
Taffeta		Soft espartra
Firm crêpe de Chine	Domette, nuns veiling Butter muslin, lawn	Millinery canvas
Tussore and shantung		Millinery net
Velvet or velveteen	Tarlatan, leno muslin, millinery net	Soft espartra, tailors or millinery canvas
Light weight tweed	Leno muslin	Do.
Stockinette		

Before cutting out, shrink the canvas and interlining, and linen, tweed or cotton materials.

3. PLACING AND CUTTING OUT. The brim is sometimes planned with a join at either side in preference to one seam at the centre-back. This cuts more

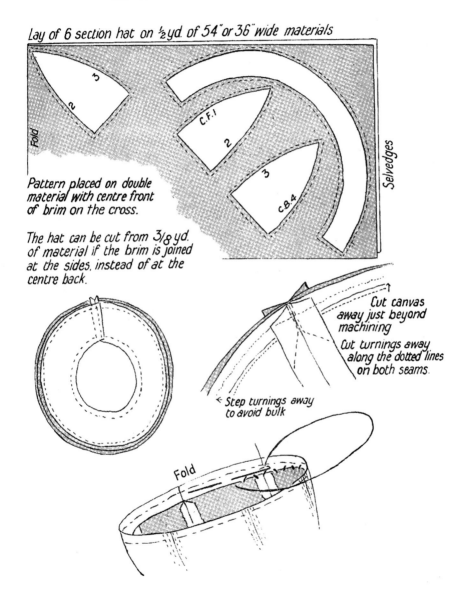

Lay of 6 section hat on ½ yd. of 54" or 36" wide materials

Fold

3

2

C.F.1

2

3

c.b.4

Selvedges

Pattern placed on double material with centre front of brim on the cross.

The hat can be cut from 3/8 yd. of material if the brim is joined at the sides, instead of at the centre back.

Cut canvas away just beyond machining

Cut turnings away along the dotted lines on both seams.

← Step turnings away to avoid bulk

Fold

economically. Care must be taken that joins on the brim and underbrim and stiffening material do not come one on the top of the other or the turnings will cause a lump in the seam. Follow the general rule for cutting out as in Chapter IV, and place the centre-front of all parts to the cross of the material. Cut an upper and underbrim, and note that they are both right side out. Cut the crown singly. For a sectional crown, either place the selvedge thread down the centre of each section or place each section on the direct cross. Note that any pattern, rib, or twill meets becomingly at the seams, and that the pile or nap smooths in a suitable direction.

TURNINGS ALLOWED. These will depend on whether the material frays badly or not. More turnings may be required.

Head: leave	$\frac{3}{4}$ in.
Brim seam: leave	$\frac{1}{4}$ in. to $\frac{1}{2}$ in.
Side seam: leave	$\frac{3}{4}$ in.
Sideband edge: leave	$\frac{1}{4}$ in.
Sectional crown: leave	$\frac{3}{4}$ in.
Tip: cut exact to size.	

ORDER OF WORK IN MAKING UP.

(a) Cut out as shown in the diagram, page 63. Mark the centre-front on brim and crown with tailors chalk or thread, and number the seams of any sections. The edge of paper pattern or the fitting lines need only be marked in pencil on the canvas or other interlining.

(b) Join up the seam or seams of all the brims. Damp well and press the seams open. All pressing must be very well done with a heavy iron as for tailoring, and superfluous turnings carefully pared away or the effect will be unprofessional.

(c) Baste the upper brim to the canvas.

Place the upper and underbrims right sides facing with the canvas on the top. Match the centre-fronts and baste firmly together, keeping all the pieces flat on the table and avoiding any "air bubbles" between. Tack and stitch by machine round the outer edge of brim. Use a large stitch and work carefully to get a perfect outline and avoid slipping. When passing over thick seams machine up to $\frac{1}{4}$ in. outside the tacking line to allow room for the turnings and avoid a drawn-in effect.

Remove the tacks. Press the turnings open, working over a roll of flannel. Trim away the interlining to nothing, snip off the corners of seam turnings. Trim the upper and underbrim turnings at the stitched seam to different widths to avoid a ridge. If desired a coronet cord or wire may be fixed to the edge now. The latter will rust if washed, the former is a washing wire. For method see Chapter III, page 17. (See Supplement illustrations.)

(d) Turn the brim right side out with the canvas inside. Tack very carefully with small stitches at the outer edge. Roll the seam slightly to the underside for a turn-down brim, and roll it over towards the upper side where the hat turns up. Tack the underbrim to the interlining at the headline, work from the centre-front in either direction. Baste the three brims carefully together. Work

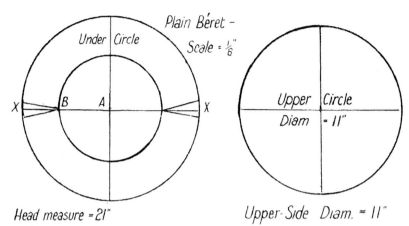

Plain Béret -
Scale = ⅙"

Under Circle

Upper Circle
Diam = 11"

Head measure = 21"

Upper-Side Diam. = 11"

Under-side **AB** = ⅙ head measure
XX = Diam. of Upper Circle + ½"
Take out a 1" dart divided equally
each side of X

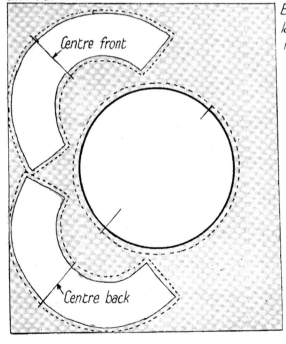

Centre front

Centre back

Béret Pattern
laid on ⅝ yrd. 18"
material —

from the outer edge and use silk to match as it may get caught in the machining. Press carefully under a damp flannel. Stitch as desired. Begin at the outer edge and use a quilter or presser foot as a guide. Test the headline (see Chapter III, page 16), correct if necessary. Snip the turnings at the head every $\frac{1}{2}$ in.

Many other little fancies may masquerade as brims on a stitched hat, and the stretched crossway method described in Chapter III, page 25 is often used for a narrow roll brim and keeps its shape well. (See illustrations in Supplement.)

Little caps are also made in stitched material with half a brim or two half brims like a fanciful deer stalker, and the reader may refer to the Boy's School Cap described on page 69.

The Crown.

SECTIONAL. Baste each section to the interlining if this is being used.

Join the sections together in such a way that the last seam runs completely from side to side or front to back. Keep exactly to the fitting lines, and note that the headlines and points always match. Press each seam as worked, and trim away the interlining to the stitching.

A frequent accident occurs here. The front is sometimes confused with the sides, therefore it should be clearly marked or the crown will not fit.

Place on the block wrong side out. Steam or damp well and press into shape with a hot iron.

Turn up the turnings at the headline of the crown. Tack. Find the four quarters on crown and brim. Place the crown over the brim, quarters matching, fitting lines touching, tack and try on. Adjust the depth of the crown as necessary. Remove the crown from the brim, mark the new headline, and trim away any interlining or turnings. Velvet hem the raw edge of the crown to the wrong side of the crown. Press on a sleeve board. Tack the crown over the brim turnings and either slipstitch or machine in position.

Another method of attaching the crown is used on a man's tweed hat. It avoids bulk from overlapping turnings on the headline.

Cut a weft way strip of material equal head measure plus 1 in. for join, by 1 in. to 2 in. wide. Join this to head size and one edge to the brim and one to the edge of crown. The join should be covered with a tailored bow or buckle and end.

A crown with tip and sideband. Cut the pattern as in Chapter II, page 9, and make up as directed in Chapter IV, page 36. Decorative stitching may be done on the tip and sideband before the two are joined together. Guiding lines should be drawn on the wrong side.

Take every precaution to avoid bulk, otherwise treat as directed in section (d) above.

Berets.

These comfortable and becoming little caps are never long out of fashion. They will vary in size, the position in which they are worn on the head, and the amount and position of the drapery, but the principle of cutting and making is the same.

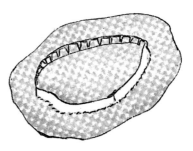

Right sides of Béret facing,
showing cloth basted to canvas.
Stitch ⅛" outside the tacking
over the seams.

Petersham ribbon joined in
circle to neaten and strengthen
head line. Turn ribbon into the
crown

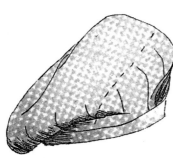

Béret.------shows
height of Bandeau- of
espartra attached at
head line only -

THE PATTERN. The original shape as worn in our childhood consists of
two circles about 10 in. to 11 in. in diameter, one of which has a circle or oval
cut out of it which equals the head size.

A better effect is obtained with the pattern drafted as illustrated on page 65.
This gives a slightly uplifted or rounded effect. Once this is understood, and if
the reader is familiar with Chapter II, it will be seen that the pattern of the
underside of a fashionable beret may be built up in the same way as a turned-up
brim. The beret may be higher at the side or back and narrower at the other
side or front. In fact any shape may be copied from a fashionable illustration.
The top of the beret will be either a circle or an oval, cut so that the outer edge
fits the edge of the underside to which it must be joined. If a circle, the radius
of the upperside will therefore be $\frac{1}{6}$ the circumference of the underside after it
is pleated up. The illustration of this type of beret will be found in the
Supplement.

If it is not fashionable to wear berets well on the head, the lifted shape at
side or back is sometimes given by inserting a bandeau between the beret and
the headlining.

Making Up Berets.

These are made with or without an interlining as the material requires.
For suitable interlinings see page 62.

WHERE THE HEADLINING AND INTERLINING ARE CUT TO THE SAME SIZE
AS THE BERET. Cut out the material, interlining and lining with the centre-
front to the cross and allow $\frac{1}{2}$ in. turnings. Mark the headline and the centre-
front, also the remaining quarters. Baste the cloth to the interlining. Join the
seams of the undercircle by machine through cloth and interlining, trim away
the interlining at the seams and press the seams open.

Join the seams of the undercircle of lining and press them open. This now
gives four pieces, i.e. two upper circles and two under circles. Place these on
the table in pairs with the right sides facing, i.e. two cloths right side facing
and two linings right side facing. Baste each pair. Place two pairs with the
wrong sides of the uppercircles facing and the two headlines visible. Baste
very carefully indeed so that they cannot slip in the machine, and stitch through
all thicknesses at the outer edge. (See note on page 64 to avoid thickness at the
seams.)

Trim away any canvas interlining at the turnings. Place the flannel roll
inside the cloth tam and press the seams open over the roll with a hot iron.
Damp the seam with a finger dipped in water if required. Trim the cloth turnings with scissors so that they are of different widths or "stepped."

Turn the undercircle of the cloth over so that its wrong side faces the wrong
side of the lining. The beret is now all right side out and lined.

Tack round the headline through all thicknesses and press the seam at
the outer edge from the right side, working with the pad inside the covering
and cover the seam with a piece of cloth. Damp if required, but sparingly,
because the headlining will watermark. Brush the seam with a clothes

brush while the steam rises. Test the head size and snip the head turnings every $\frac{1}{2}$ in.

It only remains to neaten the turnings at the head. Take a piece of petersham to tone in colour either with the hair or the beret. The piece should equal head measure plus $\frac{1}{2}$ in. and be $\frac{3}{4}$ in. to 1 in. wide. Join into a circle to fit the head by means of a strong seam. Mark the halves and quarters on both the band and the beret. Place the band to come to the headline and cover the turnings. Hem strongly in position and turn the band into the beret.

For the fashionable type of beret mentioned on page 68 and illustrated in the Supplement, it is better to make up the beret without the lining.

Insert the narrow petersham ribbon to strengthen the headline and use a cap headlining. (Chapter V, page 39.) This lining should fit the head well so that the beret does not come down too far on the head. The beret may be caught to the cap lining and so hold any drapery in place.

If the beret is made of velvet, refer to page 4, where there are hints on the use of this material.

Boy's School Cap.

Some schools supply the caps that they expect their pupils to wear, but it is very useful to be able to make an extra cap for holiday use to match the coat to be worn and to save wear and tear of the school cap. Caps take very little material, and sufficient can usually be found in the cuttings left over from the coat. If not, $\frac{1}{4}$ of a yard of 54 in. material will be sufficient, and $\frac{3}{8}$ yd. of 36 in. material for the lining.

The measurements necessary will be size of head at headline, and the side-to-side measure, taken just above the ears, and it is on these two lines that the pattern is built.

Pattern, see diagram on page 70.

$AB = \frac{1}{2}$ head measure $\qquad$ (complete oblong and mark centre-front,
$CD =$ side to side measure $\qquad$) $\qquad$ centre-back.

Divide AB into $\frac{1}{8}$th ($= \frac{1}{2}$ sections; mark these points 1, 2, 3, etc.).
Divide CD into $\frac{1}{2} = XY$.

Measure $\frac{1}{4}$ in. to left of points 3, 5, 7 to make cap fit the front of the head.
Measure $\frac{1}{4}$ in. to either side of lines 2, 4, 6, 8 on line XY.
Measure up at $A1$ $\frac{3}{4}$ in. to $1\frac{1}{4}$ in.

,, $\qquad$,, $\qquad$ $A2$ $\frac{3}{4}$ in. to 1 in.
,, $\qquad$ down at D $\frac{1}{4}$ in.
,, $\qquad$,, $\qquad$ $B2$ 1 in. to $1\frac{1}{4}$ in.
,, $\qquad$,, $\qquad$ $B1$ $1\frac{1}{4}$ in. to $1\frac{3}{4}$ in. $\qquad$ Curve the headline through these points.

Keep the line across the back section almost straight.

Make a $\frac{1}{4}$ in. dart at $B3$ to fit cut into curve of head.

THE PEAK. Draw a section of a circle with a 6 in. radius. Mark the centre-front by drawing a line at right angles to it. Measure the width of the three front sections on either side of this line $= xy$. Depth of peak at centre-front $=$

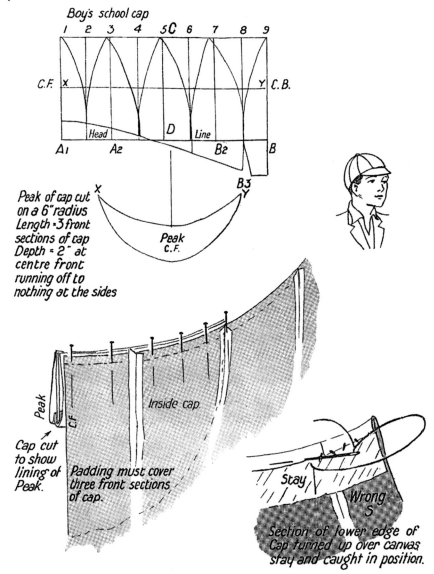

Boy's school cap

1 2 3 4 5 C 6 7 8 9

C.F. X   Y C.B.

Head   D   Line

A1   A2   B2   B

B3

Peak of cap cut
on a 6" radius
Length = 3 front
sections of cap
Depth = 2" at
centre front
running off to
nothing at the sides

Peak
C.F.

Peak

C.F.

Inside cap.

Cap cut
to show
lining of
Peak.

Padding must cover
three front sections
of cap.

Stay

Wrong

Section of lower edge of
Cap turned up over canvas
stay and caught in position.

1½ in. to 2 in., join this point to *xy* with a shallow curve, avoiding a point at the centre-front.

The materials needed are blue or grey cloth, tweed, or the material of which the coat is made. Shrink all material before using it. Polonaise for lining.

Double buckram with edges mulled, or millboard. Canvas for the stay at the head. A button covered with the material of which the cap is to be made. Large reel of silk for sewing.

To Cut the Cap. The cap is cut in eight sections with no join at the centre-front or centre-back. The headline in all sections must be cut on the cross-thread. Leave ¼ in. turning on all sections, but ½ in. at the headline.

Cut the canvas stay on the cross, the length of the head measure plus 1 in. turning and 1½ in. wide. Join into a circle.

Cut the peak, which must be mulled at the edge, as explained in Chapter III, page 18. The covering is made of double flannel, an upper and an underside, allowing ¼ in. turning at the outer edge, ½ in. at the headline. Make up as for the brim of a stitched sectional crown.

The headlining may be either a cap headlining with the tip backed with a piece of canvas, basted to the inside of the tip before making up, directions for which will be found in Chapter V, page 39, or a lining cut and made in sections in the same way as the cap. Either lining would be fixed into the hat by slip stitching when the making is complete.

To Make Up the Cap. Join the seams in pairs as for an adult sectional hat (page 66.) Tack the stay inside the cap ½ in. from the raw edge.

Pin the peak in position at the front of the cap, upper side of peak to the right side of cap.

Fix by machining.

Pad the front part of the cap from above the peak to the tip with a layer of wadding. This wadding should be thickest at the centre-front, running off to nothing at the sides. Fix lightly in place with catch stitch.

Turn up the lower edge of the cap ½ in., and catch on to the canvas stay. Press well over a pad or on a hat block. Neaten the top of the cap with a button.

Insert the headlining and fix with slip stitch.

CHAPTER IX

CHILDREN'S HATS

THE general principles which underlie the choice of children's millinery are, simplicity of style, and a soft foundation on which to make the hat. Soft light materials should be chosen, and coronet cord should be used instead of wire, which might hurt the child's tender skull.

In the case of bonnets or hats for very young children it is an advantage if they can be easily laundered. In which case the actual bonnet material, the lining, interlining, should all be shrunk before making up.

The most suitable materials for babies' bonnets and caps are—

Outer Covering	Interlining	Lining
Crêpe de Chine	Book muslin	Jap silk
Silk piqué	Book muslin	Sarcenet
Muslin		Mull muslin or unlined
Linen		Mull muslin
Lace		Net
Organdie	Unlined or double organdie	

The quantity of material necessary varies according to the type of bonnet chosen, but $\frac{1}{4}$ yd. of each lining, interlining, and covering would be sufficient for a first or second size of bonnet.

For the ties, $1\frac{1}{4}$ yd. of ribbon, $1\frac{1}{2}$ in. to 2 in. wide is necessary.

TABLE OF SIZES FOR BABIES' AND CHILDREN'S BONNETS

Age	Size round Face	Ear to Ear Back	Forehead to Back of Neck	Forehead to Crown
	In.	In.	In.	In.
Baby 1st size	12	$9\frac{1}{4}$	9	$5\frac{1}{2}$
Baby 2nd size	$14\frac{1}{2}$	10	11	5 to $5\frac{1}{4}$
2 years (small face) . . .	$15\frac{1}{2}$	10	11	5 to $5\frac{1}{2}$
3 years	16	12	$11\frac{1}{2}$	$5\frac{1}{2}$
5 years	$15\frac{1}{2}$ to 16	12	11	6
7 years	$15\frac{1}{2}$ to 16	13	$11\frac{1}{2}$	$6\frac{1}{2}$
$8\frac{1}{2}$ years	$16\frac{1}{2}$	14	$13\frac{1}{2}$	$6\frac{1}{2}$

How to take the head measure of a child

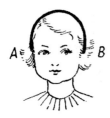

Side to side measure

Back to front measure

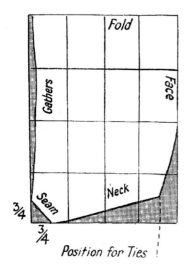

Puritan Bonnet

Bonnet with horse-shoe crown

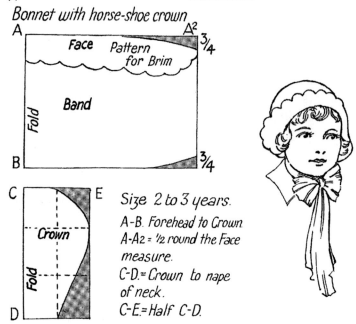

Size 2 to 3 years.

A-B. Forehead to Crown.

A-A2 = ½ round the Face measure.

C-D.= Crown to nape of neck.

C-E.= Half C-D.

Baby Boy's Hat

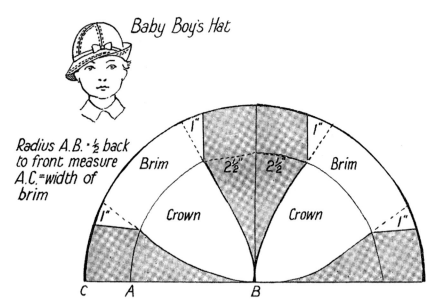

Radius A.B. · ½ back to front measure

A.C.= width of brim

The average head measure for a boy of 5 years will be about 20 in.

Directions for taking these measurements will be found in Chapter IX, page 72. The position for taking these measures will be found on page 73.

Children's heads vary in size much more than grown-ups, and it is always wiser to measure the head before starting to make the hat or bonnet.

The measurements necessary for a baby's bonnet are, round the face, and from the forehead to the nape of the neck.

Two patterns are given for babies' bonnets, one with a horseshoe crown, and one with the bonnet gathered into a small circle at the back.

Cutting Out.

Place the fold of the pattern to a selvedge fold of the material. Allow ½ in. turnings all round except for the smaller sizes, when the pattern is used without turnings. Repeat for the lining and interlining.

The button for the back should be about the size of a half-crown, and made of double leno, covered with silk.

Baste the interlining and covering together and treat as one piece. Join up the back seam of the bonnet and of the headlining. Press flat open. Pleat or gather the bonnet and join it to the button prepared for the back, keeping the larger pleats or gathers at the top of the button. Fix with slip stitch. Make up the headlining, gathering in on to the centre-back piece. Turn in the outer edges of the bonnet and catch to the interlining with loose hemming stitches.

Slip stitch the lining into the bonnet. A "cap front" or quilling may be inserted between the lining and the face.

Sew in the strings, at the corners of the bonnet, between the bonnet and the lining. The strings should be 1¼ yd. long, and are left uncut.

A brim may be liked for the bonnet. This is cut from the bonnet pattern to the shape required, of two thicknesses of the bonnet material and one thickness of leno. It is made up as the brim of an adult's stitched hat, see page 62, and inserted between the bonnet and the lining.

The second bonnet, with a horseshoe crown, is made up in the same way as the Puritan bonnet, but if liked the lower back edge may be neatened with a cross-way strip, and a draw-string inserted, to tie at the centre-back.

A horseshoe lining can be used in the first type of bonnet if preferred. The bonnet and lining are made up separately, then the lining is slip-stitched into the bonnet.

CHAPTER X

RIBBON TRIMMINGS

PETERSHAM ribbon is a firm ribbed ribbon much used in millinery. It can be obtained in nearly all colours and in widths varying from $\frac{1}{4}$ in. to 6 in. wide. Petersham ribbon must not be confused with ribbed satin ribbon which has a satin stripe down the side, or with faille ribbon, and care must be taken to buy only real silk petersham for shrinking. The artificial silk and mercerized cotton varieties will split when damped, but these are suitable for trimming, such as bows.

Petersham ribbon makes an attractive and useful trimming for hats, and is especially suitable for hard wear. It is charming made into small flat bows or folded into cockades, pleats, or knots. It can also be used to neaten and bind the outer edges of brims, either over a plain edge or else over a wire which has been previously fixed to the brim by wire stitch. (See Chapter III, page 17.)

This ribbon has one drawback. It is rather heavy, and this fact must always be considered before deciding whether it will be suitable on the hat to be trimmed.

Petersham may be shrunk to shape and then fixed to the under edge of the brim, strengthening and covering the raw edge.

To BIND AN EDGE WITH PETERSHAM.

A petersham bind is generally used to neaten an edge that has been wired. Use a narrow width petersham, not less than $\frac{1}{2}$ in. wide. Cut off a sufficient length of petersham to go round the hat, allowing $1\frac{1}{2}$ in. extra for turnings.

Place the right side of the petersham to the upper edge of the brim, turning in the raw end before starting to sew. Fix in position with backstitch, the long stitches to come on the petersham $\frac{1}{4}$ in. from the edge of the brim, and the short ones to show on the underside of the hat. The petersham must be held slightly tight all the time. When the centre-back is again reached, cut off any extra ribbon, turn in the raw end to exactly meet at the back. Slip stitch this join very carefully. Turn the petersham over on to the underside of the brim. Press very firmly under a damp cloth with a hot iron, but being very careful not to mark the petersham. Pin the edge of the petersham to come exactly on the running stitches, with pins stabbed in to avoid marking the hat. Fix in position with slip stitching. Remove pins. Give a final press under a damp cloth, from the underside of the hat, as petersham marks very easily when pressed on the right side.

To STRETCH THE PETERSHAM, place it in cold water, take it out, arrange it in a curve on an ironing sheet, wrong side up, then press with a hot iron. It will be found necessary to stretch the outer edge of the petersham at the same time that the inner edge is being shrunk. Silk petersham up to $1\frac{1}{2}$ in. in width can be treated in this way, but in the wider widths, a gathering thread must be run in at one edge before the petersham is damped, if a smaller circle is needed. It will be found impossible to shrink or stretch any but silk petersham, so care must be taken to buy the correct kind.

On a straw hat the edge of the brim must be turned in and pressed while still damp. Then the prepared petersham can be fixed in position. Apply a small quantity of millinery solution to the underside of the brim and to the petersham. Leave to get nearly dry. Then apply a second coat to both hat and ribbon.

Pin in position at centre-back, centre-front, and sides with the pins at right angles to the edge. Turn in one raw edge at the centre-back, and overlap the other edge. Press together till the solution is set. With some types of coarse straw it may be necessary to add invisible ties at frequent intervals round the outer edge or to prickstitch all round the brim.

Petersham Cockade.

An effective petersham hat ornament can be made from 2 yds. of petersham, 1¼ in. wide. A circle of double leno, 2½ in. diameter, and some muslin to neaten the edge will be also required. Also silk for sewing. The ornament consists of twelve leaves, and a centre with twelve points. The number of leaves and points can be varied by using a different width petersham, but the number of points and leaves must always be equal.

Cut the petersham in half and put 1 yd. on one side.

Place 1 yd. flat on the table.

Take the top left-hand corner and fold it over on to the lower edge to form a right angle, *AB* in diagram. Fold this right angle back under the length of ribbon to obtain a straight end.

Fold over the upper edge of ribbon to again form a right angle. Fold the length of ribbon over the top to obtain a straight edge. Continue until nearly the whole length of ribbon is used up and twelve points have been made. Put a gathering thread along the upper edge and pull up together. Join the two raw edges together with the join inside a fold.

Take the second piece of ribbon and divide it into twelve 3 in. lengths.

Fold in halves lengthways. Then fold over to form a mitre (see page 79).

Put a gathering thread along the lower edge, leaving the cotton hanging, for attaching to the circle of leno. Make up all twelve leaves.

Take the two circles of leno, and neaten the edges with a bind of cross-cut material, to match the petersham if possible.

Divide the circle into twelfths at the outer edge. Pin the twelve leaves in position with the points slightly projecting over the edge of the circle. Draw up the gathering threads until the blunt ends of the leaves fit into the inner part of the circle. When these are arranged evenly stitch in position, stabbing the stitches through the petersham and mount, using the cotton that was left hanging from the gathering.

Now take the previously made centre piece. Arrange it with the twelve points between the twelve leaves, projecting slightly beyond the edge of the leno mount. Pin in position. When arranged evenly, stitch firmly at the points but keeping the stitches hidden in a fold of the petersham, again stabbing the stitches in and out of the ribbon and the mount.

As the designs for petersham trimmings are mainly geometrical, special care must be taken that all measurements are absolutely exact, or the tailored effect sought after will be entirely lost.

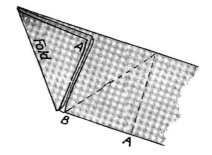

Fold the lengths of
ribbon into triangles
until twelve points
have been made.

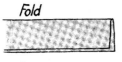

3" Length of ribbon
folded.

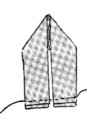

Ribbon folded to
form a mitre, with
gathering thread
for attaching to
mount.

Folded ribbon, mounted
on a circle of double
Leno, mulled at outer edge.
Size of circle 2½" diam.

BOXPLEATING.

A useful and easily made trimming is made by box pleating a length of petersham. A small piece of leno and sewing silk to match the petersham will be needed.

Take a length of the petersham and pin it down on the table. Mark it into $\frac{1}{4}$ or $\frac{1}{2}$ in. according to the size required for the finished pleat.

Pleat up the ribbon as shown in the diagram, and fix by a row of machining (see page 81), having first placed a narrow strip of leno at the back to keep the pleating firm. This may be varied by ironing down one corner of the pleats.

A double box pleat with the top pleats caught across in the centre is also useful. This is started in the same way as single box pleat by dividing the petersham into $\frac{1}{4}$ or $\frac{1}{2}$ in. according to the size pleat required.

The petersham is then folded as in diagram 4, page 81, two pleats coming exactly on the top of each other. When all the pleats are arranged in position, machine down the centre in the same way as for the single pleats.

Then take a needle threaded with silk to match the petersham, tie a knot about $1\frac{1}{2}$ in. from the end. Take a small stitch at the upper edge of the top pleat, putting the needle in from the right side. To complete the pleat take a second stitch in the lower edge of the same pleat, but this time putting the needle in from the under or wrong side, pull these two edges together, and secure with a reef knot, which will come between the two edges of ribbon and will, therefore, be hidden. Each pleat must be made separately and tied very firmly.

It is possible to make a number of varieties of this trimming, by altering the size and number of pleats, and by using two different coloured petershams.

CAN YOU TIE A BOW? The answer to this question was supposed to determine whether or no a worker had good fingers. In point of fact very few millinery bows are tied because, if they were, the ribbon would be too creased. The following directions and illustrations will show how to achieve a smart bow easily. It should be noted to begin with, that the centre of a bow is called the root, and like a woman's waist it must be neat.

The amount of material required depends on the width of the ribbon—$\frac{3}{4}$ yd. of ribbon about 3 in. or 4 in. wide makes a nice bow. A little more may be required for a 6 in. ribbon, and the worker can easily experiment by folding a tape measure to find out the amount required for a narrow ribbon. It is useful to remember that it takes just under $\frac{3}{4}$ yd. of ribbon to go round the crown of a hat.

Quilling - Allow a little more than seven times the finished length

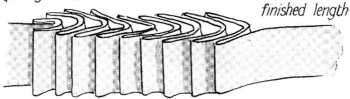

Pump Bow - Preparing -

Complete

machine

Boxpleating - Single and Double

Tie at centre

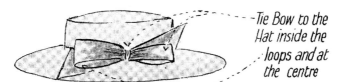

Tie Bow to the Hat inside the loops and at the centre

To Make a Tied Bow.

Cut the end of the ribbon on the slant to prevent fraying. Keep the piece cut off for use later. Pleat the ribbon about 4 in. from the end, this is the "root," bind it tightly with cotton, leave the cotton hanging. (See diagram 1.) Make the first loop. It should be a little shorter than the end. Notice that in diagram No. 1 the pleats turn towards the right, if the ribbon for the loop is placed as diagram No. 2 the next set of pleats will turn towards the left. This trick of altering the pleats at the root serves to keep the loop springy and fresh, and is always used on bows and rosettes, unless a flat effect is required, as for a Pump bow. Continue making the second loop of the tie bow as diagram No. 3. Bind tightly and tie the cotton in a reef knot. Neaten the root with the piece of slanting ribbon. Turn in the raw edges with an iron, and trim off the superfluous ribbon so that a neat strip is obtained. Bind this round the root and neaten at the back by a few hemming stitches.

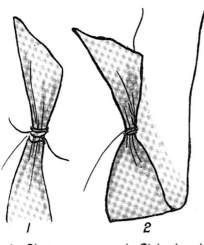

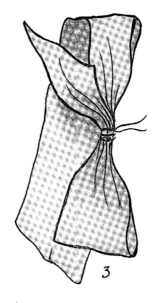

1. Pleats turn towards Right hand
2.   „   „   „   Left   „
3.   „   „   „   Right „
4. Neaten centre with small piece of silk
   folded very tightly and hemmed at the back

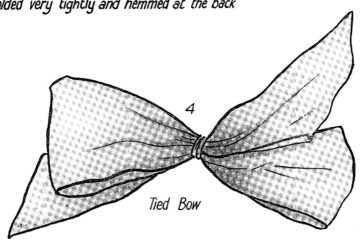

Tied Bow

A Butterfly Bow.

This takes the same amount of ribbon as a tie bow, but a crisp ribbon, such as taffeta or velvet, should be chosen, or the ends will require wiring. Cut the end of ribbon straight. Pleat the end, bind it, make a loop reversing the pleats as for the tie bow, make a second loop. The remainder of the ribbon is made into a third loop, and the root bound and neatened with a tie-over as before. Cut diagonally across the third loop from x to x (diagram 2). If the ribbon has a wrong side it will be necessary to twist one end sharply to bring the ribbon right-side out. This is a very smart bow and light in weight if made by these directions.

Butterfly bows - Cut loop from
X to X and twist one end

A Loop Rosette.

Is akin to a bow, as the loops are made in the same way, but it has several roots, while a bow only has one.

The diagrams 1 and 2, on page 87, show how the loops are made. The same piece of cotton may be carried on, and not less than seven loops should be made.

To Mount the Rosette. Take a piece of something stiff, a circle about the size of half-crown: espartra, buckram, or even stiff paper. Sew the loops to this, beginning to arrange them round the outer edge, and ending with the last loop in the centre. In fixing, stab the needle to and fro through the rosette.

A Pump Bow.

This is a simple flat bow used when a tailored effect is desired. The diagram on page 81 shows how it is made.

Pump bows are sometimes varied by pleating the ribbon across the centre. The finished bow may be very lightly pressed with a warm iron under a cloth.

To Wire Ribbon.

There are three methods in general use—

(a) Wire stitch a fine lappet wire down the centre, using sewing silk to match. Useful on velvet ribbon or narrow ribbon. The ribbon is afterwards lightly twisted to hide the wire.

(b) The ribbon is run in a narrow hem at each edge of ribbon—used on wide ribbons.

(c) A ribbon wire is made into a loop the desired shape and size. The ribbon arranged over it and tied to it by reef knots as required. The ties are, of course, inside the loops.

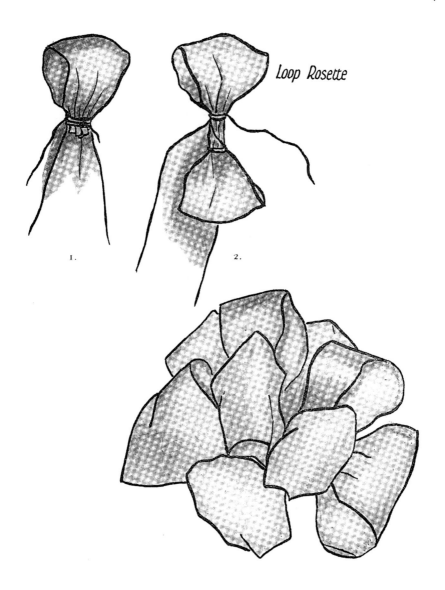

Loop Rosette

1.

2.

SUPPLEMENT

TABLE OF DIFFERENT KINDS OF STRAWS

KIND	APPEARANCE	AMOUNT IN BUNDLE or SIZE OF HOOD	SPECIAL NOTES	TREATMENT
				General caution : always test a small piece of the straw to see how it behaves when treated with damp and heat.
Rafia	Plaited in about seven strands. In natural and bright colours. Suitable for country or garden hats.	18–20 yd. bundles. Two bundles will make 3 hats of ordinary size.	Very easy to work.	Made in the hand from the tip outwards. Brim and crown worked in one. Will absorb moisture, and the straw needs damping on the wrong side as the work proceeds.
Jute	Has the appearance of hessian or sacking.		Do.	Will stand any treatment or stiffening.
Hemp	Resembles coarse canvas. It can be obtained in any colour, as well as in black and white.	Sold in hoods which vary slightly in size according to price, the more expensive ones having large brims.	Easy to handle when thoroughly wet.	Should be soaked in cold water for 2–3 hours, when it can be easily moulded over a block to fit the wearer.
Rush	Has a rough basketwork finish. Is suitable for children's hats, country or garden wear.	Can be obtained in hoods or in bundles.	Will absorb large quantities of water and then is easy to handle. When dry is inclined to break.	Must be soaked for 24 hours, and will absorb large quantities of water. This straw can then be either blocked or made in the hand according to whether a hood or bundle straw has been purchased.
Paper pulp	A straw with a rough surface. It is used frequently in inexpensive hats.	Can be bought both by the yard and in hoods.	This straw is cheap to buy but one of the most difficult to handle, as it is liable to tear when the needle is inserted in it.	As this straw is delicate it should not be put in water but moistened by holding in the steam from a kettle.

TABLE OF DIFFERENT KINDS OF STRAWS—*(contd.)*

Kind	Appearance	Amount in Bundle or Size of Hood	Special Notes	Treatment
				General caution: always test a small piece of the straw to see how it behaves when treated with damp and heat.
Horsehair and Crinolines	In appearance this straw resembles either coarse net or lace, and can also be obtained by the yard in strips of 3 plaits sewn together.	Is sold by the yard in bundles of 11 to 12 metres, or in the case of the very narrow varieties 36 yd. to the bundle. The hoods are large and have good brims.	Difficult to handle as it becomes tender and sticky when damp. Must not be over-heated or overdamped. When blocking hoods the centre of the crown has a tendency to rise when put on to the block and should be fixed down with a drawing pin before steaming or damping. Always place on a block before steaming or the shape will be lost.	Should always be steamed into shape and then stiffened with one of the preparations sold for that purpose. The lacy variety is some-times used round the outer edge of brims. If used for an entire hat the straw is usually mounted over a found-ation of blocked mil-linery net or tulle. Directions for making can be found in Chapter III, page 23.
Pedda or Dunstable straw	A fine straw plaited in England used for chil-dren's millinery.	Sold in bundles con-taining 9–12 yd.	Stiff to work. Can be damped without harm.	Is always made up on the block, working with the right side of the straw to the block, starting at the top of the crown and working down to the brim.
Chip straw	One of the cheapest kinds of straw obtain-able. It has a rough surface and is suitable for country or garden wear.	Is sold in bundles or by the yard. 8 yd. is gen-erally sufficient for an ordinary sized hat.	Easy to work and very effective for country wear.	This straw is made up in the hand as the raffia straws. By slightly oil-ing the straw during working it will be found much easier to manipu-late.
Pedaline	A glossy finished pedal straw.			

Kind	Appearance	Amount in Bundle or Size of Hood	Special Notes	Treatment
				General caution: always test a small piece of the straw to see how it behaves when treated with damp and heat.
Pedal	A fine plait straw with a dull finish. Four plaits stitched together to make the required width.	Is sold in bundles of about 10 yd. lengths.	A soft finished straw—can usually be made up without any moisture being necessary. There is often a gathering thread along one edge of the plait.	With this straw a foundation of blocked net or leno is often necessary to give the support needed for crown. The brim would be wired at the outer edge.
Tuscan } Leghorn }	Natural straws, with a slightly ribbed surface.	Always sold in the hood, which is of a good size and with a large brim.	These straws are expensive, but with care can be re-blocked very satisfactorily.	These straws need soaking in water for some hours before re-blocking.
Panama	This make of straw is always bought in the hood. It is woven from the centre to the outer edge of the brim. Usually the hoods are plain, but it is possible to obtain hoods in which some of the strands of straw have been removed, having the appearance of drawn thread work. The genuine panama comes from Central America, and is very fine.	Always sold in the hood. These vary in size according to whether the hat is to be for a man, woman, or child.	Panamas require hard work to complete, as the straw is hard and does not stretch easily, but very satisfactory when finished. These straws are valuable and will repay care. They may be cleaned at home by scrubbing with kitchen salt and lemon juice, and rinsing in cold water, then re-blocking.	As these hats are originally woven under water they will stand a great amount of soaking before blocking. From 24-36 hours, and in the case of renovations it may be necessary to keep them under water for 3 or 4 days. This will renew the straw, and render it pliable. The straw will absorb a large amount of water, and it may be necessary to refill the vessel in which the hat has been put to soak. No stiffening is necessary, as the straw stiffens as it dries.

TABLE OF DIFFERENT KINDS OF STRAWS—(contd.)

KIND	APPEARANCE	AMOUNT IN BUNDLE OR SIZE OF HOOD	SPECIAL NOTES	TREATMENT General caution: always test a small piece of the straw to see how it behaves when treated with damp and heat.
Bankok	This straw is similar in weave and appearance to panama, but has a more even appearance and a more silky finish.	Sold in the hood—real or imitation.	Requires much pulling when blocking, but is worth the trouble.	Treat as Panama. Gum may be placed in the water for stiffening purposes.
Paribuntal	A rougher type of straw than a Bankok.	Always sold in hoods, which are of a good size and a large brim.	After blocking, Pari buntal and Bankok straws will need treatment with one of the millinery varnishes sold for this purpose.	These straws may be soaked in water for a few hours before blocking.
Parisisol	This straw resembles a glazed Bankok.	Do.		
Celophane	a highly-glazed, brittle straw, always sold by the yard or in bundles. The surface can be either very rough or fairly smooth.	Is sold by the yard or in bundles containing 9–12 yd.	Owing to the brittle nature of the straws very difficult to handle, Often combined with other straws. Frays badly.	Any moisture necessary must be applied by holding in the steam of a kettle. Great care must be taken when stitching as the straw breaks away very easily. Can be made up in the hand or on a foundation of blocked net.
Chenille	Velvet thread interwoven with cotton or straw to form a plait.	Sold in bundles. Length varies according to width.	Useful for toques and caps. Usually has gathering thread in one edge.	Treat as for velvet.
French satin straw	Shiny, but not so brittle as celophane.	Usually by the bundle.	Fairly easy to handle. Usually a gathering thread in one edge.	Damp with steam lightly on the wrong side.

Kind	Appearance	Amount in Bundle or Size of Hood	Special Notes	Treatment General caution: always test a small piece of the straw to see how it behaves when treated with damp and heat.
Mottled English straw	A natural straw.	By the bundle.	Easy to work.	Damp as required.
Straw braid	Is a straw woven in various widths, from 1 in. to 4 in. The thread of the straw is woven diagonally from side to side, making it very pliable.	Sold by the yard.	Can be obtained in plain or fancy weaves, and in rough or smooth finish.	This type of straw is usually made up into small hats or toques. Any moisture necessary is obtained by holding the straw in the steam from a kettle.
Viska	A straw with a silky finish, rather like pedal in appearance, but always sold made up into hoods.	Always sold in hood form.		
Ramie	Coarse straw, sold in various colours.	Sold in bundles of 10 yds.	A cheap make of straw grown in China, woven in Switzerland.	The hat is made up in the same way as raffia plait, then placed on the block, steamed, and pressed to shape.

PATTERN MAKING

RIGHT. Soft felt hat folded and placed on double paper as described in Method 1, page 5.

CENTRE. Paper pattern drafted to direct measure as described in Method 2, page 6, and pleated to make it turn up.

LEFT. A useful way to take a pattern of a stiff brim. Crumple a sheet of soft paper. Pin smoothly round the outer edge of the brim. Allow the paper to smooth right up to the headline. Pin at headline. Take up superfluous paper at the centre back in a pleat. Pencil the outline of the brim and the headline. Mark the centre front. Remove paper from the hat. Cut on the pencilled lines. Fold the pattern in half from the centre front to find the centre back, and the pattern is then ready to place on material. Take the precaution of measuring the headline of the pattern and correcting it to the measurement of the hat.

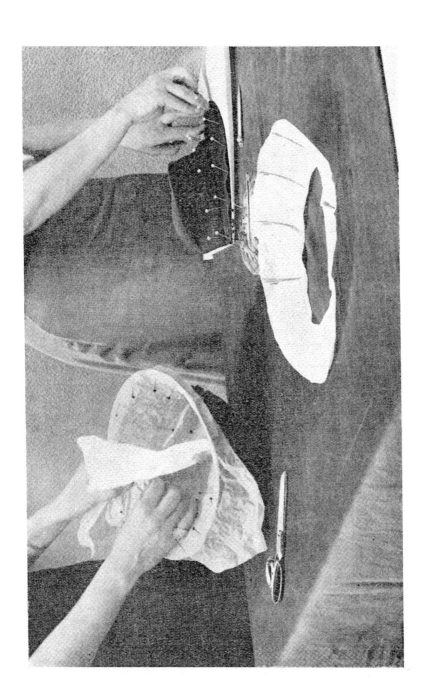

ABOVE. Measuring the headline of a finished model. Note the fingers must be close together and a very little piece measured at a time. Check the measure. It is difficult, but necessary, to be quite accurate.

BELOW. Holding the wire tight and easing the brim when wiring the edge, as described on page 18.

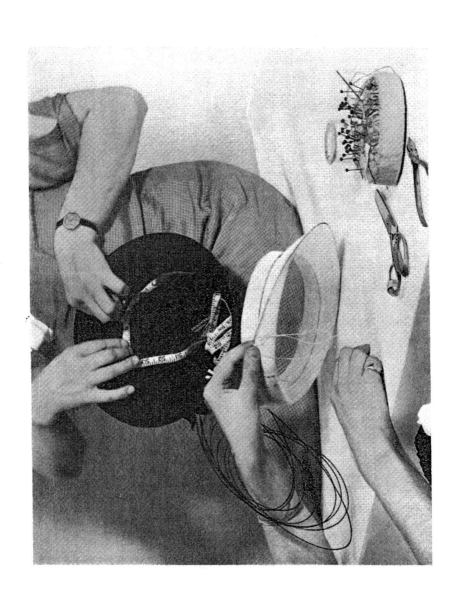

ABOVE. Moulding a curved brim by hand as described on page 20. The rounded pad is filling out the brim and is held in position by the left hand.

BELOW. Crown with moulded tip, as described on page 22.

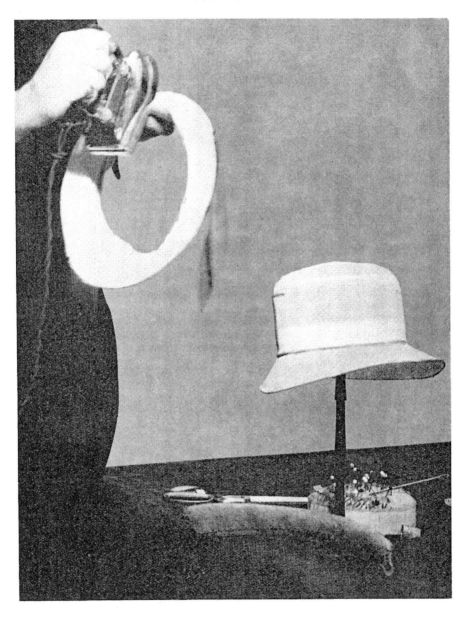

Top Left. Blocking a millinery net crown as described on page 23.

Right. The finished result.

Bottom Left. Making a small shape with brim and sideband in one piece, as described on page 24.

The wire is hanging on the left wrist, and is enclosed in the esparta which is stretched on to the wire and so spreads to form a little brim.

Finished examples of this type are shown on Plate 6.

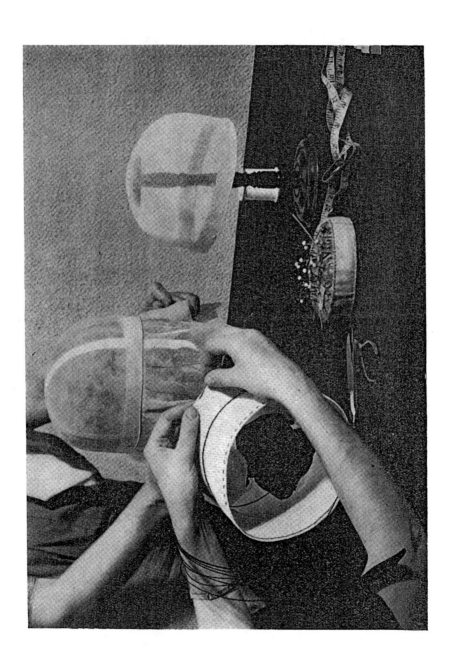

LEFT. Ironing the brim into shape on the edge of a table, as described on page 25.

RIGHT. Covering a brim as described on page 28. The direction of the thread is shown by the tack line. Pull in the same direction to remove the wrinkle.

FELT HATS

LEFT. Nigger Angora felt hat, with a 2½-in. inverted pleat on the crown running from front to back. The pleat runs out to nothing at the headline. Tack it in position, then wet the hood and block the crown.

Measurements: Front to back, 14 in. Side to side, 13½ in. Head measure, 22½ in.

Brim: Centre front, 1¾ in. ⎫
      Centre back, 3 in. ⎪
      Left-hand side, 2½ in. ⎬ outer circumference, 31 in.
      Right-hand side, 3 in. ⎭

Trimmed nigger panne velvet, tucked across the front only. Knot of felt to hold the brim up at the back.

MIDDLE. Felt hat suitable to wear with a knot of hair, with folds as described on page 47.

RIGHT. Bottle green felt with light green and beige felt inserted as described on page 46. The bands measure ½ in. wide in front to 1 in. wide at the back.

FELT HATS

Making tucks as described on page 47.

LEFT. Prick stitching to hold the string in position inside the tuck. (Note: a coarse cotton was used for purposes of illustration.)

RIGHT. The finished tucks. This toque is made with crown and brim in one piece, as described on page 47.

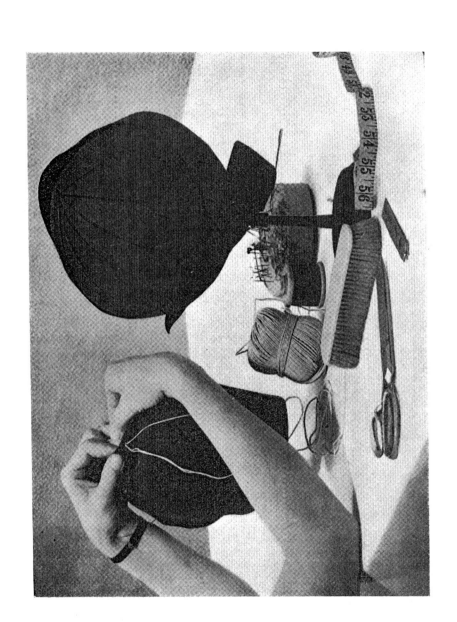

A FOLDED FELT HAT

With cover and brim in one piece, as described on page 47.

RIGHT. Hood blocked, showing how far to cut brim from crown.

LEFT. Stitching the ends to form draped ties. The block is resting against the worker's apron, and the ends are stretched hard while the hood is hot and wet.

STRAW HATS

LEFT. A picot straw hat trimmed petersham ribbon, pump bow.
Measurements: Tip $= 7\frac{1}{2}$ in. $\times$ 7 in.
Sideband, $2\frac{1}{2}$ in. Brim placed half-way up sideband.
Width of Brim: Centre front, $2\frac{3}{4}$ in.; centre back, 3 in.; left-hand side, 3 in.; right-hand side, 3 in.
Outer circumference $=$ 35 in.

CENTRE. Parisisol. The brim lifted on the left to form a bandeau and support two loop rosettes.
Width of Brim: Centre front, $2\frac{1}{2}$ in.; sides, 3 in.; centre back, $1\frac{3}{4}$ in.
See description of method on page 58.

RIGHT. Coarse straw hat of plait made as described on page 49. The crown made in one piece with the brim. Make the crown too high, and fold into a pleat when damp.

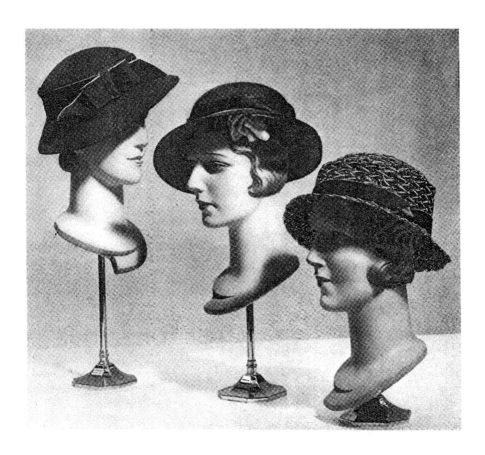

STITCHED HAT FOR A CHILD WITH SIX PIECE
SECTION AT CROWN

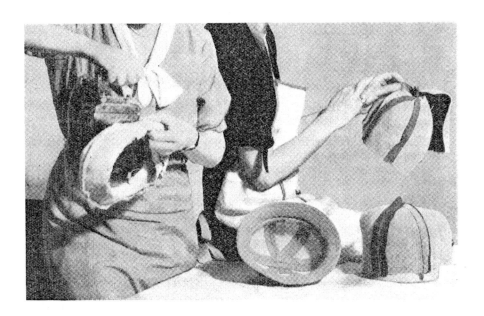

MAKING UP STITCHED HAT

LEFT. Pressing brim turnings open.

TOP RIGHT. Joining the crown. Three and three.

BOTTOM RIGHT. Crown seams. One joined; one with canvas cut away and pressed open.

CENTRE. Hat finished ready for headlining.
See notes on pages 64 and 66.

A FASHIONABLE BERET

MATERIALS REQUIRED. ⅜ yd. of 54-in. material. ¾ yd. of petersham ribbon, 1 in. wide. A feather mount.

CUTTING. Place the centre front of both under and upper circles to the cross-thread of the material.

Cut out, allowing ¾ in. turning at the headline, ¼ in. elsewhere. Mark the headline, centre front, centre back, and quarters on both circles.

To MAKE UP. Join the seam of the under circle. Press the join open. Pin the upper and underside of the circles together; right side facing, halves and quarters matching. Work with the under circle held towards the worker.

Tack and machine very accurately. See page 66 for detailed directions.

Press the join open over a roll of flannel, see Chapter VIII, page 68.

Make up a petersham band to equal the head size, using a flat join pressed open. Mark the halves and quarters. Centre front tack should be left in permanently.

Turn in the ¾ in. turnings allowed at the headline and tack. Hem the petersham band in position, ⅛ in. inside the hat. Remove tackings. Press at the headline, under a damp cloth, and over the end of a sleeve board, from the inside of the hat.

Trim with the feather mount fixed about 1 in. to the left of the centre back, neatened at the base by a small pump bow, directions for making which will be found in Chapter X, page 86.

A Fashionable Beret.

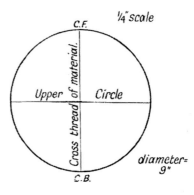

¼" scale

C.F.

Cross thread of material.

Upper | Circle

C.B.

diameter= 9"

To fit a 22" head.

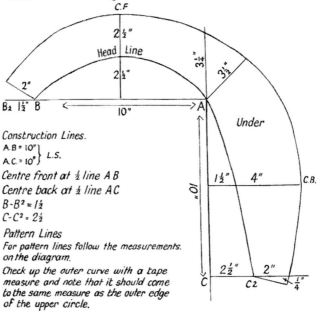

C.F

2½"

Head Line

2½"

3¼"

3½"

2"

B² 1½" B ⟵ 10" ⟶ A

Under

10"

1½" 4" C.B.

10"

2½" 2"

C C2 ¼"

Construction Lines.

A.B = 10" ⎱ L.S.
A.C. = 10" ⎰

Centre front at ½ line A B
Centre back at ½ line A C
B-B² = 1½
C-C² = 2½

Pattern Lines

For pattern lines follow the measurements.
on the diagram.

Check up the outer curve with a tape
measure and note that it should come
to the same measure as the outer edge
of the upper circle.

EXAMPLES OF STITCHED HATS

LEFT. A stitched hat, the crown made with a tip and sideband. Taffeta on felt.

CENTRE. A tweed hat. Sections run from front to back, melon fashion.
Brim in two pieces, made like peak of boy's cap and overlapping each other.

RIGHT. Sectional cap in velvet. Openwork and faggot stitched together.
Brim consists of crossway strips $1\frac{1}{2}$ in. wide. Machined and turned right side out to form a cord and faggoted together.

HAT BLOCKS

By kind Permission of Levine and Son

A 50. Modern Dome Shape Hat Pressing Block.

A 51. Hat Pressing Block, Skull Shape.

A 48. Square Shape Hat Block.

A 49. Popular Square Shape Block.

A 52. The Very Latest Improved Hat Stretcher.

A 44. Modern Standard Shape Brim Block.

A 45. Dome Shape Aluminium Hat Stretcher and Heating Block.

A 47. Patent 8 Section Expanding Hat Block.

A 46. Aluminium Skull Shape Hat Block.

A 43. Baseboard.

A 53. Rubber Cap.

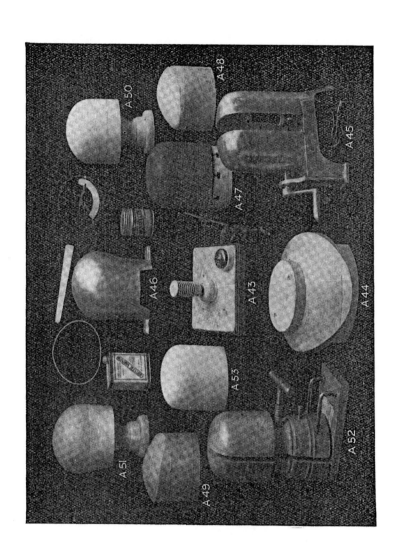

CPSIA information can be obtained
at www.ICGtesting.com
Printed in the USA
FFOW04n1354040215
10782FF